cooking for

to enjoy yourself

cooking for

to enjoy yourself

fiona williams

foulsham
LONDON • NEW YORK • TORONTO • SYDNEY

foulsham

The Publishing House, Bennetts Close, Cippenham,
Slough, Berkshire, SL1 5AP, England

ISBN 0-572-03016-9

Photographs and cover photographs by Carol and Terry Pastor

Cover photographs: Sautéed duck breast with kumquat and red onion marmalade (page 112)

Tiles for photographs supplied by Smith and Wareham Ltd Tile Merchants, Unit 2, Autopark, Eastgate Street, Bury St Edmunds, Suffolk IP33 1YQ, www.smithandwareham.co.uk

A CIP record for this book is available from the British Library

Thanks and acknowledgements
Many thanks to friends, family and colleagues who have passed on recipes that have formed the basis of some of those found in this collection. Thanks most of all to my husband, Tom, for being such a willing guinea pig.

Printed in Great Britain by St Edmundsbury Press, Bury St Edmunds, Suffolk

Contents

Introduction   7

Stylish eating and easy entertaining   8

Sample menus   11

Notes on the recipes   12

Starters   13

Poultry main courses   28

Meat main courses   43

Seafood main courses   62

Vegetarian main courses   75

Side dishes, garnishes and sauces   93

Desserts   118

Index   142

Introduction

Having friends to supper is always much more enjoyable if you can sit down with them, feeling and looking relaxed. This is fairly difficult if you've been slaving over a complicated meal for hours and it's almost impossible if you've already had a tiring day.

If – like me – you like to eat beautifully prepared, imaginative foods and enjoy the time you spend sharing meals with family and friends, but don't want to spend ages on shopping or fiddly preparation and cooking, then this book is for you.

The recipes I have brought together in this collection are the ones I have found to be the most successful for entertaining. All of them were tried and tested in the French Alps, where I catered for winter and summer chalet parties. There the number of guests varied from three to 16, making it even more important to choose recipes that were quick and simple to prepare, and which could easily be adapted for a greater or smaller number of guests. With budgets high on the agenda, it goes without saying that these recipes are economical too.

Although the ski slopes may be a far cry from your suburban kitchen, we can learn a great deal from the chalet hosts and hostesses who prepare the daily meals for those lucky enough to be taking their winter holidays. They set the very highest standards of quality and presentation, but they know from experience the best ways of serving up delicious and inspiring meals whilst keeping preparation to a minimum. Because, let's face it, part of the reason for taking the job is that they want to get out on the slopes, too!

All those factors make these recipes ideal for you as well. You can serve them for your family meals, since they are easy to create when you arrive home tired after a day's work. You can also use them when you are entertaining, as you can impress your guests with wonderful food without slaving over a complicated meal for hours or following fiendishly difficult and expensive recipes. In short, you are sure to find a range of favourites here that you'll soon have as part of your regular repertoire.

Stylish eating and easy entertaining

There is nothing magic about eating well. If you follow a few straightforward rules, it makes the whole thing really simple and irons out the hassle factor so that you can start to enjoy your cooking – and eating. That's what the chalet hosts and hostesses do! Easy entertaining and good food are more about confidence and planning than slavishly trendy recipes. The important things are to balance your menu for colour, flavour, texture and cost, select good food carefully, cook it simply and finally serve it with a flourish (even if you are a bit nervous).

A little planning goes a long way

Most people do one main shop a week, so to get the best out of it, take a little time to plan out your week's menus in advance, instead of just wandering up and down the aisles and picking up anything that takes your fancy. That way you don't end up with no meat and too much salad stuff – or whatever it is that catches your eye when you're in the supermarket. You don't have to plan everything to the letter, but just think through your ideas for the week. Then, at the very least, it will save you from that ghastly feeling when you slump in the chair after work and you have absolutely no idea of the answer to the question: 'What's for supper?'

Once you have the basics covered, it is much easier to pop out and buy a few fresh vegetables or whatever extras you need during the week.

Your storecupboard

I like to keep a well-filled storecupboard. If you build up a stock of basics, it makes it much easier to mix and match menus and you will always have something on hand to rustle up interesting meals. You won't want everything on this list – just take a look and select those things that you use on a regular basis. Make sure you replace them before you run out. Fresh fruit and vegetables should be bought as you require them.

Packets and jars
- Baking powder
- Bicarbonate of soda (baking soda)
- Biscuits (cookies) – digestive (graham crackers), amaretti, sponge (lady) fingers
- Bulghar (cracked wheat)
- Chocolate – plain (semi-sweet), milk and white
- Cocoa (unsweetened chocolate) powder
- Coffee, instant
- Cornflour (cornstarch)
- Couscous
- Dried fruit – sultanas (golden raisins), prunes
- Drinking (sweetened) chocolate powder
- Flour – plain (all-purpose) and self-raising (self-rising)
- Nuts – cashews, walnuts, almonds (ground and whole), hazelnuts (filberts)
- Pasta – shapes, tagliatelle, sheets of lasagne
- Rice – long-grain white and brown, risotto (arborio)
- Sugar – caster (superfine), granulated, soft dark brown, icing (confectioners')
- UHT cream – just in case!

Flavourings and condiments
- Capers
- Cayenne
- Chilli powder and paste
- Garlic purée (paste) – wonderful if you can't be bothered to crush fresh cloves; use about 1 cm/ ½ in per garlic clove or to taste
- Ginger – fresh and preserved stem, in syrup
- Herbs, dried – basil, bay leaves, chives, dill (dill weed) oregano, rosemary, thyme, tarragon, mint, sage, mixed herbs and bouquet garni sachets
- Herbs, fresh – parsley and coriander (cilantro), for garnishing, plus any from the list of dried (above)
- Honey, clear
- Jam (conserve) – apricot, black cherry and redcurrant jelly (clear conserve)
- Lemon juice – not vital but a bottle will keep in the fridge for ages and is better than vinegar in many recipes
- Marmite or other yeast extract
- Mustard – made English, Dijon and wholegrain
- Oil – sunflower and olive, plus speciality ones like sesame and walnut for flavouring

- Olives
- Passata (sieved tomatoes)
- Pepper – black peppercorns in a mill and ready-ground white
- Pesto, ready-made
- Salt
- Sauces – Worcestershire, Tabasco and soy, plus chilli if you like hot, spicy food
- Spices – ground paprika, ginger and mace, nutmegs (they are best freshly grated), cumin and coriander (cilantro) seeds, cinnamon sticks
- Stock cubes or powder – vegetable, chicken, beef, fish
- Tomato purée (paste)
- Vinegar – red or white wine or cider, balsamic, malt

Cans
- Fish – anchovies, tuna
- Fruit – pear halves, peaches, pineapple
- Golden (light corn) syrup
- Ham
- Pulses – red kidney beans, haricot (navy) beans, chick peas (garbanzos), etc.
- Sweetcorn (corn)
- Tomatoes
- Black treacle (molasses)

Fridge and freezer
- Butter, salted and unsalted (sweet) and/or margarine
- Cream – single (light), double (heavy), soured (dairy sour), crème fraîche
- Eggs
- Bread loaves, rolls, pitta breads, naan, etc. – store in the freezer and take out when required
- Cheese – Cheddar, Mascarpone and Parmesan
- Fruit juices
- Yoghurt – Greek-style and plain
- Milk – cartons of milk can be frozen but they take ages to thaw and will need a good shake once defrosted
- Pastry (paste) – puff, shortcrust (basic pie crust)
- Fruit and vegetables, frozen – raspberries, spinach, peas and beans

Healthy eating

A healthy diet is one that provides the body with everything it needs and not too much that it doesn't. Three meals a day is a good starting point, without over-indulging (too often!) or eating too late at night, when your body doesn't have time to digest the food. Eat plenty of fresh fruit and vegetables; we should all be eating five portions a day. Use as much fresh produce as you can and avoid too many ready-made or highly processed foods, which lose their nutrients in the process. Don't add too much salt when you are cooking; use herbs and other flavourings or just let the natural flavours of the food shine through! As for sugar and sweet things, we all know that we don't **need** them at all – they are just empty calories – but I, for one, wouldn't dream of missing out on my sweet treats from time to time, so I just keep them in balance.

Choosing the food

When cooking for friends, just apply the same rules as you do to your everyday cooking for yourself and the family. Easy entertaining and good food are more about confidence and planning than spending more time and money than you can afford!

The important things to remember are:
- Balance your menu for colour, flavour and texture.
- Keep costs at a level you are comfortable with.
- Select good-quality basic ingredients.
- Cook simply and retain the basic flavours.
- Think about good presentation.
- Do as much as possible in advance.
- Serve with a flourish!

So the first thing to do is to choose a well-balanced menu, and there is a whole range of samples on page 11. Plan your time so you have everything to hand and can do as much as possible in advance, then you only have the last-minute touches to add when your guests have arrived.

Setting the scene

Presentation makes a big difference to our enjoyment of a meal, and that includes the surroundings as well as the dishes themselves. Here are a few simple tips on how to set the atmosphere – and the table.

- Lay a clean, plain tablecloth or table mats on the table.
- To arrange your place settings, start from the outside and work in, knives and spoons on the right, forks on the left. (Knife blades, by the way, face inwards as it's impolite to point your knife blade at your neighbour!)
- Set out paper or linen napkins. Either fold attractively and lay on the side plate or fold into a triangle, turn in the two corners and place in the wine glass.
- Place your glasses at the top right of each place setting. If it's formal, you may want to provide different glasses for each course.
- Add a decorative centrepiece. Fresh flowers or candles work well, but don't make it too large or too high otherwise there'll be no room for the food and your guests won't be able to see each other across the table.
- Turn the lighting down to a subtle level, but take care not to make it so dark your guests cannot see what they are eating.
- Quiet background music helps to break the ice and add atmosphere.
- Make sure the rooms are warm but not too hot. Remember that your guests will get warmer during dinner with all the good food and wine.
- Don't offer too many nibbles before dinner – it will dull your guests' appetites – but do provide something, perhaps a few fancy nuts or crisps (chips), to make sure they are not drinking their aperitifs on a completely empty stomach!
- Have enough crockery so you don't have to wash up rapidly in between courses.

Serving drinks

I always find it embarrassing when someone asks simply: 'What would you like to drink?' in case I ask for something they don't have! If you have a completely stocked bar, that's fine, otherwise the best way is to offer your guests a specific choice. You may like to keep to wine and beer, or perhaps sherry, a cocktail, or even a Buck's Fizz (champagne and orange juice). Always make sure you have plenty of mineral water and a selection of soft drinks.

There are conventions about which wine you serve with each type of food, based on flavours that complement each other, and you can use them to help you to select suitable wines for your meal. The purists suggest that with starters, fish and white meat, you should serve dry white wine. For game, red meat and cheese, a red wine, usually fuller-bodied, is considered best, and if you want to serve wine with dessert, you should choose a sweet white wine. Highly spiced foods, such as curry, are best with lager. However, I think the most important rule is that you serve whatever you most enjoy with whatever you like! Allow about half a bottle per person, and always offer mineral water and a non-alcoholic alternative.

After dinner, you can offer liqueurs, port or brandy with coffee, or just continue with wine. For many of us, a cup of good coffee and an after-dinner mint chocolate are the perfect end to a meal.

Sample menus

It is important that your meal should consist of dishes that look good, taste great and offer complementary flavours. Here are a few sample menus, using recipes from this book, that fulfil all those requirements. The recipe page numbers are in brackets.

Spanish chorizo salad with tomatoes and spring
    onions (p.25)
Spiced beef casserole with orange and rum (p.53)
Potato patties (p.108), Fried peas with garlic (p.101)
Fruit sabayon (p.125)

Orange and carrot soup with cinnamon (p.15)
Italian lamb with parma and pesto (p.55)
Garlic rosti (p.109), Orange-glazed turnips (p.112)
Frozen coffee crunch soufflés (p.128)

Grilled avocados with bacon (p.20)
Feuilletés de St Jacques (p.70)
Buttered new potatoes, Tomato salad
Hot raspberry brûlée (p.120)

Fresh tomato soup with Mediterranean herbs (p.16)
Spinach and ricotta parcels (p.90)
Potato stacks (p.109), Warm bean salad (p.94)
Poached pears with hot fudge sauce (p.131)

Seafood soup with fennel and leek (p.17)
Peppered duck breasts with cognac (p.39)
Antibes potatoes (p.108), Refried beans (p.94), Warm
    spinach salad (p.111)
Iced fruit parfait (p.138)

Spinach and Mascarpone soup with croûtons (p.14)
Leek and goats' cheese pie with tomato sauce (p.85)
Baked fennel with fresh tomatoes (p.103), Green
    salad
Coffee cream syllabub (p.126)

Fried goats' cheese with walnuts (p.27)
Potato gratin with chilli (p.77)
Steamed cauliflower with almonds (p.99),
    Garlic carrots and courgettes with lime (p.99)
Whisky oranges with honeyed cream (p.132)

Fried mushrooms with port and walnuts (p.23)
Glazed salmon with hoisin and ginger (p.65)
Potato patties (p.108), Warm bean salad (p.94)
Brandy chocolate roulade (p.130)

Smoked mackerel salad with orange and dill (p.26)
Mustard chicken with tarragon cream (p.31)
Antibes potatoes (p.108), Sweetcorn,
    Braised leeks in vermouth (p.104)
Raspberry pavlova (p.139)

Creamed courgette soup with tomato and basil (p.18)
Pescada a la marina (p.64)
Lemon potatoes (p.105), Mixed salad
Chocolate and pear pie (p.123)

Spinach and Mascarpone soup with croûtons (p.14)
Mushroom pilaff with cashew nuts (p.92)
Tomato salad, Soy garlic beans (p.96)
Baked apples with almond (p.124)

Ginger dip prawns (p.19)
Flemish beef carbonnade with a garlic crust (p.52)
Baked potatoes, French beans with onions and garlic
    (p.95), Turkish fried carrots (p.98)
Almond pear flan (p.122)

Piquant mushrooms on garlic toasts (p.24)
Sautéed trout fillets with lemon butter sauce (p.67)
New potatoes, Green salad
Chocolate and ginger trifle (p.133)

Asparagus and salmon risotto (p.21)
Roast leg of lamb with red wine and ginger (p.61)
Roast potatoes, Creamy courgette bake (p.100),
    Baby carrots with orange and cardamon (p.98)
Coffee torte with praline (p.129)

Spanish prawns with chilli and almonds (p.22)
Lemon pork tenderloin with sherried mushrooms
    (p.46)
Boiled rice, Green salad
Champagne chocolate flutes with lacy caramel webs
    (p.134)

Notes on the recipes

- Do not mix imperial, metric and American measures. Follow one set only.
- American terms are given in brackets.
- All spoon measures are level: 1 tsp = 5 ml;
                                            1 tbsp = 15 ml.
- Ingredients are listed in the order in which they are used in the recipe.
- Eggs are medium unless otherwise stated.
- Fresh produce should be washed, peeled, cored and seeded, where necessary.
- Seasoning and the use of strongly flavoured ingredients, such as onions and garlic, are very much a matter of personal preference. Taste the food and adjust the seasoning as you cook.
- Always use fresh herbs unless dried are specifically called for. If you do use dried, use only half the quantity stated. Chopped, frozen varieties are much better than dried but only fresh varieties can be used for garnishing.
- Can and packet sizes are approximate and will depend on the particular brand.
- Use butter or margarine, as you prefer, although check that any margarine you are using is suitable for cooking.
- Use your own discretion in substituting ingredients and personalising the recipes. Make notes of particular successes as you go along.
- Use whichever kitchen gadgets you like to speed up preparation and cooking times: mixers for whisking, food processors for grating, slicing, mixing or kneading, liquidisers for blending, etc.
- All ovens vary, so cooking times have to be approximate. Adjust cooking times and temperatures according to manufacturer's instructions.
- Always preheat a conventional oven and cook on the centre shelf unless otherwise specified. Fan ovens do not need preheating.

starters

Your chosen starter should set the scene for the whole dinner party. It should whet your guests' appetite for what is to follow – not dull it completely. It is also important that it complements the main course. I have given sample menus (page 11) to help you with this, but as a general rule avoid similar ingredients or similar cooking methods. For instance, you wouldn't serve Piquant Mushrooms on Garlic Toasts followed by Fillet Steaks with Creamy Mushrooms and Tarragon. Equally, you wouldn't offer your guests a soup followed by a casserole. Try to mix and match, offering a variety of flavours, textures and colours throughout the meal.

Spinach and Mascarpone soup with croûtons

What a gift of a recipe this is, using simple, readily available ingredients.
The combination of flavours is a delight to the taste buds and the result is a very
attractive dish that will really impress.

SERVES 4

30 g/1¼ oz/2½ tbsp unsalted
(sweet) butter

1 onion, chopped

2 celery sticks, chopped

350 g/12 oz fresh or thawed
frozen spinach

750 ml/1¼ pts/3 cups vegetable stock

250 g/10 oz/1¼ cups
Mascarpone cheese

Salt and freshly ground black pepper

FOR THE CROÛTONS
1 small garlic clove

A pinch of dried rosemary

45 ml/3 tbsp olive oil

4 thick slices of white bread, diced

1 Melt the butter in a large pan. Add the onion and celery and cook gently for about 5 minutes until softened but not browned.

2 Add the spinach to the pan, then pour in the stock and bring to the boil.

3 Reduce the heat, cover and simmer for 15–20 minutes.

4 Blend the soup in a liquidiser or food processor until smooth and return to the pan.

5 Add the Mascarpone and gently reheat, adding salt and pepper to taste.

6 To make the croûtons, crush the garlic and rosemary using a pestle and mortar and gradually add the oil. Pour the flavoured oil over the bread cubes and stir until well coated.

7 Grill (broil) until golden brown and crunchy.

8 Serve the soup in warm bowls, with a few croûtons sprinkled over the surface.

Preparation and cooking time 25–30 minutes

Orange and carrot soup with cinnamon

This wonderful, orange-flavoured soup makes a fabulous warming start to any meal. The orange complements the sweet taste of the carrots and both give the soup a lovely, bright colour.

SERVES 4

Finely grated rind of 1 orange

1 onion, finely chopped

450 g/1 lb carrots, chopped

5 mm/¼ in piece of fresh root ginger, peeled and finely chopped

5 cm/2 in piece of cinnamon stick

750 ml/1¼ pts/3 cups chicken stock

200 ml/7 fl oz/scant 1 cup fresh orange juice

Salt and freshly ground black pepper

60 ml/4 tbsp plain yoghurt

1 egg yolk

TO GARNISH
Orange zest, cut into matchsticks

1 Place all the ingredients except the yoghurt and egg yolk into a saucepan. Bring to the boil and simmer for 25 minutes.

2 Cool the soup slightly, then discard the cinnamon stick and liquidise in a blender or food processor until smooth. Return to the rinsed-out pan.

3 Beat the yoghurt and egg yolk together, add a little of the soup and stir, then return all this mixture to the pan. Heat through gently, but do not boil.

4 Serve hot, garnished with matchsticks of orange zest.

Preparation and cooking time 40 minutes

Hints and variations This soup is also delicious served chilled.

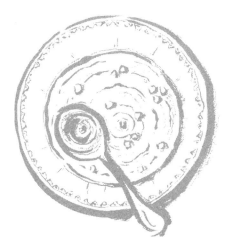

Fresh tomato soup with Mediterranean herbs

This tasty soup contains lots of lovely fresh vegetables as well as the tomatoes, making it not only very tasty but very healthy too. The fresh herbs add a special fragrance that will whet your guests' appetites.

SERVES 4

30 ml/2 tbsp olive oil

2 red onions, chopped

1 carrot, chopped

2 celery sticks, chopped

500 g/18 oz fresh tomatoes, halved

750 ml/1¼ pts/3 cups vegetable stock

15 ml/1 tbsp chopped fresh oregano

15 ml/1 tbsp chopped fresh basil

150 ml/¼ pt/⅔ cup dry white wine

A pinch of caster (superfine) sugar

1 ciabatta loaf

10 ml/2 tsp tomato purée (paste)

15–30 ml/1–2 tbsp
Worcestershire sauce

Salt and freshly ground black pepper

TO GARNISH
Sprigs of fresh basil

1 Heat the oil in a large pan, add the onions, carrot and celery and fry (sauté) gently until softened but not browned.

2 Add the tomatoes, stock, herbs, wine and sugar. Bring to the boil, then reduce the heat, cover and simmer gently for 20 minutes.

3 Warm the ciabatta bread in a preheated oven at 190°C/375°F/gas 5/ fan oven 170°C for 3–4 minutes.

4 Liquidise the soup in a blender or food processor; add the tomato purée and Worcestershire sauce, and season to taste with salt and pepper.

5 Reheat and garnish with the basil sprigs.

6 Serve with the warmed ciabatta.

Preparation and cooking time 30–35 minutes

Hints and variations This recipe can be part-prepared in advance up to the end of Step 2. This can help you in the evening when you have lots of other dishes to prepare, plus it is always easier to blend the soup when it is no longer boiling hot.

Seafood soup with fennel and leek

This very easy soup is always a winner at dinner parties – for the cook as well the guests – because so little effort is required for such a gorgeous result. Saffron is expensive but I like to use it as it adds such a subtle flavour.

SERVES 4

30 ml/2 tbsp sunflower oil

1 small onion, chopped

½ bulb of fennel, sliced

½ leek, sliced

15 ml/1 tbsp plain (all-purpose) flour

150 ml/¼ pt/⅔ cup dry white wine

600 ml/1 pt/2½ cups skimmed milk

450 g/1 lb seafood cocktail, fresh or frozen

A pinch of saffron strands

2.5 ml/½ tsp dried dill (dill weed)

Salt and freshly ground black pepper

1 Heat the oil in a saucepan and add the chopped onion, fennel and leek. Sauté until softened but not browned, then stir in the flour and cook for 1 minute.

2 Add the wine, bring to the boil, then reduce the heat and simmer for 2 minutes.

3 Add the milk, seafood cocktail, saffron and dill, and season with salt and pepper. Heat gently for 10–15 minutes until piping hot.

Preparation and cooking time 15–20 minutes

Creamed courgette soup with tomato and basil

This is a very quick and easy soup to make (and inexpensive too), yet it tastes really rich and is very filling. When you are using basil, treat it very gently as it bruises and damages easily.

SERVES 4

25 g/1 oz/2 tbsp butter or margarine

1 onion, finely chopped

3 courgettes (zucchini), coarsely grated

1 garlic clove, crushed

600 ml/1 pt/2½ cups vegetable stock

400 g/14 oz/1 large can of chopped tomatoes

15 ml/1 tbsp tomato purée (paste)

30 ml/2 tbsp fresh basil leaves, torn

Salt and freshly ground black pepper

TO GARNISH

60 ml/4 tbsp double (heavy) cream

A few fresh basil leaves

1 Melt the butter or margarine in a large pan. Add the onion and cook until softened but not browned. Add the courgettes and garlic and cook for 3–4 minutes.

2 Add the stock, tomatoes and their juice and the tomato purée. Bring to the boil, then reduce the heat, cover and simmer for 15 minutes. Add the torn basil leaves and season to taste with salt and pepper.

3 Ladle into warm soup bowls and serve garnished with a swirl of cream and a few leaves of fresh basil.

Preparation and cooking time 30 minutes

Hints and variations If you have time, prepare the soup in advance, to give the flavours time to develop, then reheat when ready to serve.

Ginger dip prawns

This is an easy starter that is best prepared well in advance so that the flavours have time to develop. When I am entertaining, that makes it ideal as it gives me more time to enjoy with my guests.

SERVES 4

200 ml/7 fl oz/scant 1 cup plain Greek yoghurt

A dash of single (light) cream

1 garlic clove, crushed

5 ml/1 tsp grated fresh root ginger

5 ml/1 tsp wholegrain mustard

5 ml/1 tsp Worcestershire sauce

16 cooked peeled tiger prawns (jumbo shrimp)

TO GARNISH
Wedges of lemon

Sprigs of fresh parsley

TO SERVE
Warm granary bread

1 Mix together the yoghurt, cream, garlic, ginger, mustard and Worcester sauce.

2 Cover and chill for an hour or so to allow the flavours to develop.

3 Divide the dip among four little ramekin dishes (custard cups) and put each one on the centre of a side plate.

4 Arrange the prawns around.

5 Decorate with wedges of lemon and sprigs of parsley and serve with warm granary bread.

Preparation and cooking time 10 minutes plus chilling

Hints and variations If you can't find big tiger prawns, use more of the smaller variety.

19

Grilled avocados with bacon

Here is an ideal starter for big appetites on cold evenings – the golden-brown baked avocado and bacon mixture looks and smells delicious. Remember not to leave the chopped avocado standing otherwise it will brown.

SERVES 4

25 g/1 oz/2 tbsp butter or margarine, plus a little extra

25 g/1 oz/¼ cup plain (all-purpose) flour

300 ml/½ pt/1¼ cups milk

50 g/2 oz/½ cup Cheddar cheese, grated

100 g/4 oz cooked bacon, chopped

2 ripe avocados

30 ml/2 tbsp fresh breadcrumbs

1 Melt the butter or margarine in a pan, add the flour and cook for 1 minute before gradually adding the milk and bringing to the boil. Remove from the heat and stir in the cheese and cooked bacon.

2 Peel the avocados, remove the stones (pits) and chop the flesh into chunks. Add to the cheese and bacon mixture. Spoon into ramekins (custard cups) or if you prefer you can use the avocado skins. Sprinkle with the breadcrumbs and dot with small flakes of butter or margarine to prevent the tops being too dry.

3 Put under a hot grill (broiler) until browned and bubbly.

Preparation and cooking time 10 minutes

Serving suggestions Arrange on individual plates on a bed of your favourite fresh salad leaves and serve with brown bread and butter or crusty rolls.

Asparagus and salmon risotto

This risotto is a real treat with its luxury ingredients of smoked salmon and asparagus. You can buy off-cuts of smoked salmon, which are much cheaper but ideal for this dish. The grated lemon rind lightly offsets the richness.

SERVES 6

50 g/2 oz/¼ cup butter or margarine

30 ml/2 tbsp chopped fresh dill (dill weed)

2.5 ml/½ tsp grated lemon zest

30 ml/2 tbsp olive oil

3 shallots, sliced

225 g/8 oz fresh asparagus spears, sliced

275 g/10 oz/1¼ cups risotto (arborio) rice

300 ml/½ pt/1¼ cups dry white wine

900 ml/1½ pts/3¾ cups hot vegetable stock

Salt and freshly ground black pepper

100 g/4 oz smoked salmon, cut into strips

TO GARNISH
Chopped fresh parsley

1 Blend 40 g/1½ oz/3 tbsp of the butter or margarine with the dill and lemon zest and set aside.

2 Heat the remaining butter or margarine in a frying pan (skillet) with the oil. When hot, add the shallots and fry (sauté) gently for 5 minutes. Add the asparagus and cook for another 5 minutes, stirring the mixture.

3 Add the rice, moving it around until all the grains are coated with the buttery mix.

4 Pour in the wine and let it bubble over a moderate heat, stirring, until it has been absorbed.

5 Add a quarter of the stock and stir over the heat until it has been absorbed by the rice. Continue adding the rest of the stock and cooking in the same way until it has all been absorbed. This process takes about 20 minutes.

6 Season to taste with salt and pepper, then remove from the heat and add the salmon strips.

7 Cover and leave for 5 minutes.

8 Stir in the flavoured butter or margarine, sprinkle with a little chopped parsley and serve.

Preparation and cooking time 40 minutes

Spanish prawns with chilli and almonds

Chilli and prawns always go well together, and the almonds add an unusual nutty element to the complementary flavours, as well as thickening the sauce to a lovely consistency.

SERVES 4

25 g/1 oz/2 tbsp butter or margarine

30 ml/2 tbsp olive oil

25 g/1 oz/¼ cup ground almonds

1 red chilli, seeded and finely chopped

1 garlic clove, finely chopped

350 g/12 oz raw prawns (shrimp), peeled

Grated rind and juice of ½ lemon

TO GARNISH

30 ml/2 tbsp chopped fresh coriander (cilantro)

1 Melt the butter or margarine in a frying pan (skillet) with the oil, then add the almonds, chilli and garlic. Cook for 2 minutes.

2 Add the prawns and lemon rind and juice, and cook over a moderate heat, stirring, until the prawns are cooked through.

3 Spoon on to warm plates and serve garnished with chopped coriander.

Preparation and cooking time 10 minutes

Hints and variations This also makes a good main course for two people, served on a bed of plain boiled rice.

Piri piri prawns

This is very spicy starter, but you can reduce the amount of chilli powder to suit your taste if you prefer your food a little milder. See photograph opposite page 24.

SERVES 4

5 ml/1 tsp chilli powder

2.5–5 ml/½–1 tsp salt

Juice of 1 small lemon or 1 lime

750 g/1¾ lb raw tiger prawns (jumbo shrimp), shelled but tails left on

A little sunflower oil, for cooking

TO GARNISH

Wedges of lemon or lime

1 Combine the chilli powder, salt and lemon or lime juice. Marinate the prawns in this mixture for 1 hour.

2 Lift out of the marinade, using a slotted spoon. Fry (sauté) for 3–4 minutes in a little hot oil until just turning pink. Be careful not to overcook.

3 Serve piping hot, garnished with lemon or lime wedges.

Preparation and cooking time 10 minutes plus marinating

Fried mushrooms with port and walnuts

This may sound like an unusual combination of flavours, but do give it a try – it really works! It is quite a rich flavour, and the walnuts add a welcome crunchy texture to the mushroom mixture.

SERVES 8

75 g/3 oz unsmoked lardons

35 g/1½ oz/2½ tbsp butter or margarine

3 medium onions, chopped

3 garlic cloves, crushed

1 kg/2¼ lb mushrooms, cleaned and sliced

5 ml/1 tsp mixed dried herbs

1 bay leaf

A pinch of freshly grated nutmeg

5 ml/1 tsp caster (superfine) sugar

5 ml/1 tsp Worcestershire sauce

Salt and freshly ground black pepper

A dash of Tabasco sauce

½ bottle of port

50 g/2 oz/¼ cup tomato purée (paste)

100 g/4 oz/1 cup walnuts, roughly chopped

1 Fry (sauté) the lardons in the butter or margarine for 2–3 minutes, then add the onions and garlic and continue to fry gently until softened.

2 Add the mushrooms, herbs, bay leaf, nutmeg, sugar, Worcestershire sauce, salt, freshly ground black pepper and a dash of Tabasco. Pour in the port and boil rapidly until reduced to a quarter of its quantity.

3 Stir in the tomato purée and remove the bay leaf.

4 Add the walnuts to the mixture and serve immediately.

Preparation and cooking time 20 minutes

Hints and variations These mushrooms are delicious served in small bowls with fresh bread or as a topping for toast. They also make a perfect filling for vol-au-vent cases.

Piquant mushrooms on garlic toasts

As well as a starter, these make a delicious hot snack or light lunch, served with a fresh salad. When you are serving your meals, do remember that presentation is very important so arrange the food beautifully on the plates.

SERVES 6

FOR THE GARLIC TOASTS
30 ml/2 tbsp olive oil

A pinch of dried mixed herbs

1 garlic clove, crushed

12 slices French bread

FOR THE PIQUANT MUSHROOMS
450 g/1 lb button mushrooms, halved

10 ml/2 tsp coriander seeds, crushed

1 red onion, sliced

60 ml/4 tbsp olive oil

90 ml/6 tbsp red wine

15 ml/1 tbsp red wine vinegar

30 ml/2 tbsp clear honey

TO GARNISH
Snipped fresh chives

1 Prepare the toasts by mixing together the oil, herbs and garlic. Brush this mixture all over the slices of bread and toast on both sides under a hot grill (broiler). Keep warm.

2 Fry (sauté) the mushrooms, coriander and onion in the oil over a high heat for 2 minutes. Cover and cook for a further 2 minutes. Add the wine, vinegar and honey. Continue to cook, stirring, for 2 minutes until the sauce is reduced.

3 Spoon on to the hot toasts and serve garnished with snipped chives.

Preparation and cooking time 15–20 minutes

Photograph opposite:
Piri Piri Prawns (see page 22)

Spanish chorizo salad with tomatoes and spring onions

This is a substantial and delicious salad. The sweet, crunchy almonds add an interesting contrast of textures and flavours. The spicy Spanish sausage, chorizo, is now readily available in supermarkets.

SERVES 6

225 g/8 oz chorizo, cut into thin slices

45 ml/3 tbsp olive oil

1 garlic clove, crushed

15 ml/1 tbsp balsamic vinegar

350 g/12 oz mixed salad leaves

Salt and freshly ground black pepper

2 plum tomatoes, chopped

6 spring onions (scallions), finely chopped

30 ml/2 tbsp flaked (slivered) almonds, toasted

1 Fry (sauté) the chorizo in the oil until just starting to crisp. Add the garlic and continue cooking. When the chorizo is crisp, remove from the heat.

2 Add the vinegar and stir, then pour over the salad leaves in a large bowl. Season with salt and pepper and scatter over the tomatoes and spring onions.

3 Toss the ingredients together, sprinkle with the toasted almonds and serve at once.

Preparation and cooking time 15 minutes

Hints and variations Try varying the salad by substituting streaky bacon for the chorizo. You could also try adding chopped hard-boiled (hard-cooked) eggs or avocado.

Photograph opposite:
Smoked Mackerel Salad with Orange and Dill (see page 26)

Smoked mackerel salad with orange and dill

*Smoked mackerel has a lovely flavour that combines well with the orange to make a
very fresh-tasting salad. See photograph opposite page 25. You can use any
smoked fish in the recipe to ring the changes.*

SERVES 6

**175 g/6 oz/1½ cups bulghar
(cracked wheat)**

900 ml/1½ pts/3¾ cups vegetable stock

2 oranges

**350 g/12 oz smoked mackerel fillets,
skinned and flaked**

30 ml/2 tbsp chopped fresh parsley

**30 ml/2 tbsp chopped fresh dill
(dill weed)**

4 spring onions (scallions), chopped

FOR THE DRESSING
45 ml/3 tbsp olive oil

Juice and grated zest of 1 orange

5 ml/1 tsp clear honey

Salt and freshly ground black pepper

TO GARNISH
Wedges of lemon

Sprigs of fresh dill

1 Simmer the bulghar in the stock for 15–20 minutes, until most of the
stock has been absorbed. Drain and cool a little.

2 Remove the skin and pith from the oranges and cut into segments.
Mix together the bulghar, orange segments and mackerel, then add
the parsley, dill and spring onions.

3 Whisk together the oil, orange juice and zest and honey, then season
to taste with salt and pepper. Pour the dressing over the salad and
toss. Chill for at least 30 minutes, so that the flavours develop.

4 Garnish with wedges of lemon and sprigs of dill.

Preparation and cooking time 30 minutes plus chilling

Serving suggestions Serve with brown bread and butter.

Hints and variations For a more substantial dish, suitable for lunch or
supper, serve with crusty bread and a tomato salad.

Fried goats' cheese with walnuts

Cheese and walnuts are natural partners, and in this dish the apricot jam adds a welcome sweet fruitiness to counteract their sharper flavours. The recipe uses the small, round goats' cheeses.

SERVES 8

2 round goats' cheeses, about 225 g/8 oz each

175 g/6 oz/½ cup apricot jam (conserve)

60 ml/4 tbsp plain (all-purpose) flour

Salt and freshly ground black pepper

50 g/2 oz/½ cup walnuts, chopped

100 g/4 oz/2 cups fresh white breadcrumbs

30 ml/2 tbsp snipped fresh chives

30 ml/2 tbsp chopped fresh parsley

1 egg, lightly beaten

50 g/2 oz/¼ cup butter or margarine

90 ml/6 tbsp oil

225 g/8 oz mixed salad leaves

1 Spread each cheese with the apricot jam. Mix the flour with some salt and pepper and use to coat the cheeses.

2 Mix together the walnuts, breadcrumbs, chives and parsley.

3 Dip the cheeses in the beaten egg and then the breadcrumb mixture. Chill for at least 15 minutes.

4 Heat the butter or margarine and oil and fry (sauté) the cheeses on both sides until golden brown.

5 Arrange the salad leaves on individual plates.

6 Cut the cheeses into quarters, place on the salad leaves, then serve.

Preparation and cooking time 15 minutes plus chilling

poultry main courses

Dinner parties should be a pleasure for the cook as well as the guests. All these main courses are simple to make. Most can be prepared in advance, then just finished at the last minute.

Golden chicken with piquant caper relish

The relish makes this simple fried chicken taste and look really special.
That's one of the features you'll find common to all my recipes – great flavour but
minimal fuss!

SERVES 6

3 anchovy fillets, drained

2 garlic cloves, crushed

2.5 ml/½ tsp balsamic vinegar

15 ml/1 tbsp capers

60 ml/4 tbsp chopped fresh parsley

150 ml/¼ pt/⅔ cup olive oil

Freshly ground black pepper

**6 chicken breast fillets,
about 175 g/6 oz each**

25 g/1 oz/2 tbsp unsalted (sweet) butter

15 ml/1 tbsp sunflower oil

1 Purée the anchovies, garlic, vinegar, capers and parsley in a blender or food processor until well combined.

2 Gradually add the olive oil, running the machine all the time. Season with pepper.

3 Fry (sauté) the chicken breasts in the butter and oil for 5–6 minutes on each side until cooked through.

4 Serve with the relish.

Preparation and cooking time 15 minutes

Serving suggestions Place each breast on a plate with a spoonful of the relish, and serve with sautéed potatoes, broccoli and carrots.

Lemon chicken with rosemary and chilli

These chicken breasts have a lemony fragrance with a spicy twist, which I think is absolutely delicious. If you prefer the dark meat, you could make the recipe with chicken legs instead.

SERVES 4

4 boned skinless chicken breasts, about 175 g/6 oz each

120 ml/4 fl oz/½ cup lemon juice

30 ml/2 tbsp chopped fresh rosemary

5 ml/1 tsp chilli paste

Salt and freshly ground black pepper

30 ml/2 tbsp olive oil

60 ml/4 tbsp soft brown sugar

1 Place the chicken breasts in a shallow, non-metallic dish.

2 Pour over the lemon juice, sprinkle with rosemary and dot with chilli paste, then season with salt and pepper. Turn the breasts to coat them all over. Cover and leave to marinate in the fridge for at least 4 hours, preferably overnight.

3 Heat the oil and fry (sauté) the breasts on a high heat, turning frequently, until browned and cooked through.

4 Pour in the marinade juices and let the mixture bubble. Add the sugar and stir until dissolved and starting to caramelise.

5 Serve the chicken on warm plates with the marinade poured over.

Preparation and cooking time 20 minutes plus marinating

Serving suggestions Arrange a bed of Creamed Spinach (page 111) on each plate, top with a chicken breast and some of the marinade and serve with sautéed potatoes.

Mustard chicken with tarragon cream

This sumptuous chicken dish has a sophisticated and delicate flavour, yet is quick and easy to prepare. Be careful when you are heating cream: keep the heat to a minimum so that it warms through without risk of curdling.

SERVES 4

4 boneless chicken breasts, about 175 g/6 oz each

25 g/1 oz/2 tbsp unsalted (sweet) butter

10 ml/2 tsp plain (all-purpose flour)

2.5 ml/¹/₂ tsp salt

1.5 ml/¹/₄ tsp freshly ground black pepper

2.5 ml/¹/₂ tsp dried tarragon

5 ml/1 tsp French mustard

120 ml/4 fl oz/¹/₂ cup white wine

120 ml/4 fl oz/¹/₂ cup double (heavy) cream

1 Fry (sauté) the chicken breasts in the butter for about 20 minutes, turning occasionally, until cooked through. Remove from the pan and keep warm.

2 Add the flour, salt and pepper, tarragon and mustard to the pan. Gradually pour in the wine, stirring all the time. Bring to the boil and let the mixture bubble until reduced by half.

3 Add the cream, then return the chicken breasts to the pan, with any juices. Cook for a further 5–6 minutes over a gentle heat.

4 Place each breast on a warm plate and pour the sauce over.

Preparation and cooking time 35–40 minutes

Serving suggestions These are excellent with Roast Potatoes Flavoured with Mustard (see page 117), Turkish Fried Carrots (page 98) and Warm Bean Salad (page 101).

Chicken and chorizo sauté with crème fraîche and cumin

This is a great one-pan supper dish for easy entertaining. It's a truly international recipe that many of my guests have enjoyed, with its Spanish chorizo, North African harissa and Indian cumin.

SERVES 4

30 ml/2 tbsp olive oil

500 g/18 oz potatoes, cut into chunks

6 button (pearl) onions

2 garlic cloves

2.5 ml/½ tsp chilli powder

1–2 chicken breasts, cut into small pieces

2 small chorizo sausages, chopped

30 ml/2 tbsp tomato purée (paste)

15–30 ml/1–2 tbsp hot chilli or harissa paste

30–45 ml/2–3 tbsp dry sherry

Salt and freshly ground black pepper

45 ml/3 tbsp crème fraîche

15 ml/1 tbsp cumin seeds, toasted

TO GARNISH

Sprigs of fresh parsley

Wedges of lemon

1 Put the oil in a large frying pan (skillet) and fry (sauté) the potatoes pieces with the whole button onions and garlic cloves for about 10 minutes.

2 Sprinkle the chilli powder over the chicken pieces and stir them into the potato mixture. Add the chopped chorizo and mix in the tomato purée, chilli or harissa paste and the sherry. Season with salt and pepper.

3 Simmer for 10 minutes until the chicken is cooked and tender.

4 When ready to serve, add the crème fraîche and sprinkle with the toasted cumin seeds.

5 Serve garnished with sprigs of parsley and wedges of lemon.

Preparation and cooking time 30 minutes

Serving suggestions There is no real need for extra vegetables with this dish, though a cool crisp salad with some warm bread rolls – ciabatta for example – would round it off nicely.

Oriental marinated chicken with cumin and ginger

This marinade is perfect for chicken as it imparts juiciness as well as flavour to the meat, and creates a delicious sweet–sharp coating. You can substitute chicken legs or wings, or it works very well with pork.

SERVES 6

45 ml/3 tbsp soy sauce

45 ml/3 tbsp clear honey

Juice of 2 oranges

1 garlic clove, crushed

15 ml/1 tbsp finely chopped fresh root ginger

10 ml/2 tsp soft brown sugar

75 ml/5 tbsp sunflower oil

5 ml/1 tsp ground cumin

6 chicken breasts, about 175 g/6 oz each

1 Put all the ingredients except the chicken into a bowl and mix together, then pour over the chicken. Leave to marinate for several hours, or overnight if possible, turning over occasionally.

2 Lift out of the marinade with a slotted spoon and bake in a preheated oven at 180°C/350°F/gas 4/fan oven 160°C for 45 minutes.

3 Serve on warm plates.

Preparation and cooking time 50 minutes plus marinating

Serving suggestions This goes well with some oriental-style accompaniments, such as stir-fried vegetables and egg noodles.

Chicken breasts and ham with melted cheese

This recipe has been a long-standing favourite with both me and my guests. It's easy to prepare, delicious and versatile, too, as it can be finished off in the oven if you find you are short of space on the hob.

SERVES 4

4 boned skinless chicken breasts, about 175 g/6 oz each

Butter or margarine and oil, for cooking

15 ml/1 tbsp chopped fresh parsley

4 slices of ham

8 mushrooms, sliced

150 ml/¹/₄ pt/²/₃ cup chicken stock

4 slices of Gruyère (Swiss) cheese

1 Fry (sauté) the chicken on each side in a little butter or margarine and oil until browned.

2 Top each with a little parsley, a slice of ham and sliced mushrooms.

3 Add the chicken stock. Cover and simmer until cooked through.

4 Top each breast with a slice of cheese. Cover again and cook until the cheese melts.

Preparation and cooking time 35 minutes

Serving suggestions I like to serve this with roast potatoes, sweetcorn (corn) and broccoli.

Chicken breasts with port and basil

Basil is a wonderfully fragrant herb and I like to keep a pot on the kitchen window sill so that I can simply pick it fresh from the plant and use it straight away. Otherwise, it tends to wilt if you do not use it quickly enough.

SERVES 4

4 boned skinless chicken breasts, about 175 g/6 oz each

Salt and freshly ground black pepper

50 g/2 oz/¼ cup butter or margarine

2 onions, sliced

1 garlic clove, chopped

225 g/8 oz/1 small can of tomatoes

75 ml/5 tbsp port or sherry

10 ml/2 tsp dried basil

60 ml/4 tbsp chopped fresh parsley

5 ml/1 tsp soft brown sugar

1 Rub the chicken breasts with salt and pepper and fry (sauté) in half the butter or margarine for 30 minutes, turning occasionally, until cooked through.

2 In a separate pan, cook the onions in the remaining butter or margarine for 2–3 minutes, then add the garlic and cook for a further 2–3 minutes. Add the tomatoes and cook for 10 minutes.

3 Stir the port or sherry, basil, parsley and sugar into the tomato mixture and bring to the boil. Add the chicken, reduce the heat, cover, and simmer for 10 minutes.

4 Serve on warm plates with the sauce poured over.

Preparation and cooking time 55 minutes

Serving suggestions Antibes Potatoes (page 108), Turkish Fried Carrots (page 98) and Fried Peas with Garlic (page 101) make good accompaniments.

Flambéed brandy chicken in a creamy mustard sauce

This delicious dinner party dish is absolutely effortless – simply serve with a flourish! Flambéing the chicken burns off the alcohol and just leaves the delicious brandy flavour in the sauce.

SERVES 4

4 chicken breasts, about 175 g/6 oz each

25 g/1 oz/2 tbsp butter or margarine

75 ml/5 tbsp brandy

FOR THE SAUCE
300 ml/½ pt/1¼ cups double (heavy) cream

15 ml/1 tbsp French mustard

Salt and freshly ground black pepper

A pinch of paprika

150 ml/¼ pt/⅔ cup chicken stock

1 In a large frying pan (skillet), fry (sauté) the chicken breasts in the butter or margarine until golden brown.

2 Pour the brandy over and light it to flambé the chicken pieces.

3 Add all the sauce ingredients and bring to the boil.

4 Reduce the heat, cover and simmer for 20 minutes, then serve.

Preparation and cooking time 30 minutes

Serving suggestions This needs only the plainest of accompaniments, such as boiled potatoes and French (green) beans.

Hints and variations If you do want to zip up the accompaniments, fry the beans in butter with a little chopped onion.

Italian-style chicken with rosemary and garlic

Golden-brown roasted chicken skin always looks wonderfully appetising, and in this recipe the crispness is a good textural contrast to the moist white meat, which is beautifully tenderised by the vinegar.

SERVES 6

6 boned chicken breasts, skin left on, about 175 g/6 oz each

2 garlic cloves, chopped

15 ml/1 tbsp olive oil

Salt and freshly ground black pepper

6 sprigs of fresh rosemary

6 rashers (slices) of streaky bacon

50 ml/2 fl oz/¼ cup red wine vinegar

1 Slash the flesh of the chicken breasts several times with a sharp knife. Rub the chopped garlic and olive oil over them and put them into a shallow roasting tin (pan). Season well with salt and pepper.

2 Lay the rosemary sprigs on top and the bacon rashers between the portions. Pour over the wine vinegar.

3 Cook on the top shelf of a preheated oven at 220°C/425°F/gas 7/fan oven 200°C for 10 minutes.

4 Reduce the heat to 200°C/400°F/gas 6/fan oven 180°C and cook for another 35 minutes, until the chicken breasts are golden brown and cooked through.

5 Transfer the chicken to warm plates and pour over any cooking juices.

Preparation and cooking time 45 minutes

Serving suggestions Serve with Italian Vegetable Bake (page 114).

Turkey escalopes in ginger wine and lemon

*Ginger wine is a rather old-fashioned drink but it makes a rich and delicious sauce –
try it with chicken or veal. A tot in a glass of whisky makes a great drink for a cold
winter evening too!*

SERVES 8

8 turkey escalopes

30 ml/2 tbsp olive oil

**100 g/4 oz/½ cup unsalted
(sweet) butter**

300 ml/½ pt/1¼ cups ginger wine

20 ml/4 tsp lemon juice

10 ml/2 tsp chopped stem ginger

90 ml/6 tbsp double (heavy) cream

Salt and freshly ground black pepper

1 Gently fry (sauté) the escalopes in the oil and butter for 5–6 minutes.
Lift on to a serving dish and keep warm.

2 Add the ginger wine to the pan and bring to the boil. Reduce the
heat and simmer for 5 minutes until the wine is syrupy.

3 Stir in the lemon juice, stem ginger and cream. Simmer for
2–3 minutes until the sauce is a pale coffee colour. Season to taste
with salt and pepper, then pour over the escalopes and serve.

Preparation and cooking time 20 minutes

Serving suggestions These tasty escalopes are good with quite plain
vegetable accompaniments; try them with roast potatoes, carrots
and buttered French (green) beans.

Hints and variations You can buy jars of preserved stem ginger;
make sure you drain off all the syrup before chopping.

Peppered duck breasts with cognac

Duck breasts have a rich, dense meat so a small amount satisfies even the healthiest appetite, making them more economical than you might think! You should cook duck so that it is slightly pink and still moist inside.

SERVES 6

90 ml/6 tbsp black peppercorns, coarsely crushed

6 small duck breasts, skin removed

Salt

45 ml/3 tbsp sunflower oil

45 ml/3 tbsp unsalted (sweet) butter

300 ml/¹⁄₂ pt/1¹⁄₄ cups cognac

300 ml/¹⁄₂ pt/1¹⁄₄ cups duck or chicken stock

300 ml/¹⁄₂ pt/1¹⁄₄ cups double (heavy) cream

1 Press the peppercorns into the duck breasts and season with a little salt.

2 Fry (sauté) in the oil and butter for 4–5 minutes on each side. Remove from the pan and keep warm.

3 De-glaze the pan with the cognac and stock. Stirring well, bring to the boil and reduce the liquid by half. Add the cream and heat gently.

4 Pour the sauce over the duck, then serve.

Preparation and cooking time 20 minutes

Serving suggestions I like to serve this with Creamed Spinach (page 111), Antibes Potatoes (page 108) and fried mushrooms.

Hints and variations The peppercorns should be just crushed, not finely ground.

Grilled duck breasts with caramelised onions

The caramelised onions can be made in advance and stored in the fridge. They are also good to serve with roast pork, cold meats, or even stirred into a casserole to give it a bit of extra flavour. See photograph opposite page 48.

SERVES 4

25 g/1 oz/2 tbsp butter or margarine

15 ml/1 tbsp sunflower oil

6 onions, thinly sliced

50 g/2 oz/¼ cup caster (superfine) sugar

30 ml/2 tbsp red wine vinegar

10 ml/2 tsp chopped fresh thyme

Salt and freshly ground black pepper

4 duck breasts

A little sunflower oil

TO GARNISH
Sprigs of fresh rosemary

1 Heat the butter or margarine and oil in a pan. Add the onions, part-cover with a lid and cook very gently for about 40 minutes, stirring regularly, until golden and tender.

2 Stir in the sugar, vinegar, thyme and salt and black pepper to taste. Cook, uncovered, for a further 20 minutes, stirring frequently until the mixture becomes thick and sticky.

3 Rub salt and pepper into the duck breasts, and grill (broil) them, skin-side up, until well browned. Turn them over and brush with a little oil and continue cooking for another 5–10 minutes, depending on their size and your preference. Season with salt and pepper and leave to rest for 5 minutes.

4 Slice the duck thinly and arrange on plates with the warm caramelised onions.

Preparation and cooking time About 1½ hours

Serving suggestions To complete the dish, serve with Garlic Rosti (page 109) and Cabbage with Nutmeg (page 97).

Sautéed duck breasts with port and redcurrant

This dish has everything – it's simple to make, it's ready in minutes and it tastes wonderfully rich. When presenting the dish, fan out the slices to display them beautifully and perhaps scatter over a few fresh redcurrants, if available.

SERVES 4

Salt and freshly ground black pepper

2 large duck breasts

90 ml/6 tbsp port

15 ml/1 tbsp redcurrant jelly (clear conserve)

TO GARNISH
Sprigs of fresh watercress

1 Sprinkle a hot frying pan (skillet) with salt, then add the duck breasts, skin-side down. Cook gently for 5 minutes. Turn over and cook for 5 minutes more. Remove from the pan and keep warm, skin-side up.

2 Add the port to the pan and boil to reduce by half. Stir in the redcurrant jelly until dissolved. Season with salt and pepper.

3 Cut the duck into thick slices and add to the sauce. If the slices are too rare for your taste, cook for another minute. Taste the sauce. If it is too sweet or too thick, add a little more port.

4 Garnish with sprigs of watercress before serving.

Preparation and cooking time 15–20 minutes

Serving suggestions I like to serve Creamed Spinach (page 111) and roast potatoes tossed in mustard (see page 117) with these – the dark green colour of the spinach contrasts particularly well with the rich red sauce.

Moroccan-style quail with saffron and sultana sauce

Quails are readily available in every supermarket in the Savoie region of France where I work and they're not expensive either. You can buy them in most major supermarkets. See photograph opposite page 49.

SERVES 6

6 quail

A little unsalted (sweet) butter, melted

Salt and freshly ground black pepper

12 shallots

15 ml/1 tbsp olive oil

150 g/5 oz/scant 1 cup sultanas (golden raisins)

Juice of 1 lemon

2 pinches of ground cumin

2 pinches of saffron strands

1 Place the quail in a roasting tin (pan), brush lightly with the butter, sprinkle with salt and freshly ground black pepper and roast in a preheated oven at 220°C/425°F/gas 7/fan oven 200°C for 30 minutes.

2 Peel the shallots and cut into quarters. Heat the olive oil in a saucepan, add the shallots and fry (sauté) gently until softened but not browned. Add the sultanas, lemon juice, cumin and saffron, then season with salt and pepper.

3 Pour in 300 ml/½ pt/1¼ cups of water and leave to simmer for about 30 minutes.

4 Remove the quail from the oven and place on a serving dish. Pour over the saffron and sultana sauce.

Preparation and cooking time 1¼ hours

Serving suggestions Serve with generous portions of creamy mashed potatoes and carrots or broccoli.

Hints and variations Most recipes advise two birds per person but I think one is enough especially when served with this sauce and plenty of potatoes. If you're lucky enough to have access to truffles, you can use a few shavings of these to enrich the mashed potatoes but of course this can blow the budget!

meat
main courses

I love entertaining, but I want to spend the maximum time with my guests – not stirring things in the kitchen while I can hear everyone laughing and enjoying themselves around the table! If you spend just that little bit of extra time planning your menu, you'll have a range of dishes that perfectly complement each other – and you can prepare as much as possible in advance. A simple dish that is beautifully prepared and presented by a relaxed hostess will impress your guests far more than a more complicated dish that leaves you hot, red-faced and harassed!

Italian-style pork chops with Mozzarella

It is always good to find a new recipe for the humble pork chop, and this is a very good one that makes an economical and delicious feast of flavours. The pork is kept moist by the topping of creamy buffalo Mozzarella cheese.

SERVES 2

30 ml/2 tbsp olive oil

2 boneless pork chops

Salt and freshly ground black pepper

30 ml/2 tbsp pesto

50 g/2 oz/½ cup Mozzarella cheese, sliced

2 plum tomatoes, quartered

15 g/½ oz stoned (pitted) black olives, chopped

1 Heat the oil in a frying pan (skillet) and fry (sauté) the pork chops for 5–8 minutes on each side, until browned and cooked through. Remove from the pan and place in a flameproof dish.

2 Season each chop with salt, then spread the pesto over the top and cover with slices of Mozzarella cheese.

3 Arrange the tomatoes and olives around the chops. Place under a preheated medium grill (broiler) for 6–8 minutes until the Mozzarella has melted and started to brown and the tomatoes are soft.

4 Add a grinding of fresh black pepper and serve immediately.

Preparation and cooking time 30–35 minutes

Serving suggestions I like to serve this with Warm Spinach Salad (page 111) and lots of crusty bread to mop up the juices.

Rolled pork tenderloin with pine nut stuffing

The unusual stuffing in these moist rolls of pork provides a fabulous variety of tastes and textures – sweet and sour, moist and nutty. Cooking the meat in the tomato sauce keeps it very moist.

SERVES 6

6 slices of pork tenderloin, about 100 g/4 oz each

Salt and freshly ground black pepper

100 g/4 oz/1 cup chopped raw cured ham, such as Westphalian, Parma, Serrano, etc.

25 g/1 oz/¼ cup pine nuts, chopped

50 g/2 oz/⅓ cup sultanas (golden raisins), chopped

45 ml/3 tbsp fresh breadcrumbs

50 g/2 oz/½ cup capers, rinsed and dried

45 ml/3 tbsp olive oil

30 ml/2 tbsp white wine

45 ml/3 tbsp passata (sieved tomatoes)

1 green chilli, seeded and finely chopped

1 Beat the pork slices until very thin. Season well with salt and pepper.

2 Mix together the ham, nuts, sultanas, breadcrumbs and capers and spoon on to the pork.

3 Roll up and secure with cocktail sticks (toothpicks).

4 Place the rolls in a frying pan (skillet) and brown in the olive oil.

5 Add the wine, passata and chilli. Reduce the heat and simmer very gently for 2 hours.

6 Transfer the rolls to warm plates, pour the sauce over and serve.

Preparation and cooking time 2¼ hours

Serving suggestions Set the rolls on a bed of plain pasta ribbons, with some fried (sautéed) courgettes (zucchini) on the side.

Lemon pork tenderloin with sherried mushrooms

I like to marinate the meat overnight but, when time is short, 30 minutes would be enough to give the meat a definite flavour. Since tenderloin has no fat, it works well when cooked in a sauce to keep it moist and full of flavour.

SERVES 6

750 g/1¾ lb pork tenderloin

30 ml/2 tbsp olive oil

15 ml/1 tbsp lemon juice

Freshly ground black pepper

1 garlic clove, crushed

FOR THE SAUCE

50 g/2 oz/¼ cup unsalted (sweet) butter

1 onion, finely sliced

175 g/6 oz button mushrooms, finely sliced

30 ml/2 tbsp dry sherry

Salt and freshly ground black pepper

150 ml/¼ pt/⅔ cup double (heavy) cream

1 Cut the meat into 2 cm/¾ in slices. Lay them between sheets of clingfilm (plastic wrap) or greaseproof (waxed) paper and beat flat with a rolling pin. Arrange the slices in a shallow dish.

2 Mix together the oil and lemon juice, season with pepper, add the garlic and spoon this marinade over the meat. Leave for a minimum of 30 minutes or preferably overnight, turning occasionally.

3 Melt the butter and fry (sauté) the onion until softened but not browned.

4 Add the mushrooms and fry for 3 minutes. Remove from the pan with a draining spoon and keep warm.

5 Drain the pork from the marinade and fry gently in the pan for 3–4 minutes, turning once. Transfer to a serving dish and keep warm.

6 Add the sherry to the pan and boil rapidly until it reduces by half. Return the onions and mushrooms to the pan with salt and pepper to taste. Stir in the cream and heat gently. Remove from the heat and pour over the pork.

Preparation and cooking time 25 minutes plus marinating

Serving suggestions Serve on a bed of rice with a crisp green salad.

Baked pork steaks with a crisp nut and mustard topping

This is quite a versatile recipe for which you can use pork chops or steaks or, better still, slices of tenderloin. You can vary the topping ingredients, depending on what you have in your storecupboard.

SERVES 8

8 pork chops or steaks

20 ml/4 tsp mustard powder

45 ml/3 tbsp soft brown sugar

30 ml/2 tbsp salted peanuts, chopped

10 ml/2 tsp Worcestershire sauce

10 ml/2 tsp white wine vinegar

5 ml/1 tsp salt

10 ml/2 tsp butter or margarine, melted

1 Grill (broil) the pork on both sides until nearly cooked.

2 Mix all the other ingredients together and spread over the meat. Place under a hot grill (broiler) to cook until they are golden brown. Alternatively, bake in a preheated oven at 200°C/400°F/gas 6/fan oven 180°C for about 20 minutes, until the topping is just golden brown.

3 Serve hot.

Preparation and cooking time 35 minutes

Serving suggestions This goes well with French Beans with Feta and Sun-dried Tomatoes (page 96), Potato Stacks (page 109) and carrots.

Hints and variations You can either grill or fry (sauté) and then bake the meat – the choice is yours.

Beef carpaccio with salsa verde

Carpaccio is usually not cooked at all. However, here it is given a quick blast in a very hot oven, which is all it needs. Make sure you don't overcook it otherwise it will become tough.

SERVES 6

FOR THE CARPACCIO
450 g/1 lb beef fillet

90 ml/6 tbsp olive oil

30 ml/2 tbsp soy sauce

Freshly ground black pepper

FOR THE SALSA
3 anchovy fillets, drained

2 garlic cloves, crushed

2.5 ml/½ tsp balsamic vinegar

15 ml/1 tbsp capers

60 ml/4 tbsp chopped fresh parsley

150 ml/¼ pt/⅔ cup olive oil

1 Slice the beef very finely (see note below), then put the thin slices under clingfilm (plastic wrap) and beat them with a rolling pin or meat mallet so they are nearly transparent.

2 Mix together the olive oil, soy sauce and plenty of black pepper and pour this marinade over the meat. Leave for a minimum of 2 hours, preferably overnight. Turn the meat over occasionally, if possible, to ensure an even coating with the marinade.

3 Meanwhile, purée all the salsa ingredients except the oil in a blender or food processor. Gradually add the oil, running the machine all the time, and season to taste with pepper.

4 Lay the drained beef slices in a single layer on two large baking (cookie) sheets. Bake in a preheated oven at 240°C/475°F/gas 9/fan oven 215°C for 1–2 minutes until the slices are just turning brown.

5 Transfer immediately to warm plates and dress with a little of the salsa.

Preparation and cooking time 12 minutes plus freezing and marinating

Serving suggestions Pasta tossed with butter and black pepper and French (green) beans make good accompaniments.

Hints and variations The beef has to be sliced really thinly and I have found the best way to do this is to freeze it until it is fairly solid, then you can slice it quite easily with a sharp knife.

Photograph opposite:
Grilled Duck Breast with Caramelised Onions (see page 40) with Garlic Rosti (see page 109) and Cabbage with Nutmeg (see page 97)

Braised beef fillet with pink peppercorns and redcurrant jelly

Beef cooked like this has a rich and fruity flavour and is amazingly tender. If you can use pink peppercorns, you'll get the added benefit of the lovely colour, but ordinary black pepper works well too.

SERVES 6

550 g/1¼ lb beef fillet, cut into 6 slices

20 pink peppercorns, lightly crushed OR plenty of coarsely ground black pepper

30 ml/2 tbsp olive oil

5 shallots, finely chopped

50 g/2 oz streaky bacon rashers (slices), rinded and cut into strips

50 g/2 oz smoked bacon rashers, rinded and cut into strips

175 ml/6 fl oz/¾ cup red wine

50 ml/2 fl oz/3½ tbsp beef stock

15 ml/1 tbsp lemon juice

A good pinch of freshly grated nutmeg

30 ml/2 tbsp redcurrant jelly (clear conserve)

Salt and freshly ground black pepper

1 Sprinkle both sides of the beef slices with crushed pepper.

2 Heat the oil and seal the beef on each side. When browned, remove from the pan and keep warm.

3 Add the shallots and streaky and smoked bacon pieces to the pan and fry (sauté) for 4–5 minutes.

4 Stir in the wine, stock, lemon juice and nutmeg. Bring to the boil, add the redcurrant jelly, stirring until dissolved, and season with salt and pepper.

5 Replace the meat and simmer for about 5–10 minutes until the meat is tender.

6 Serve the meat on warm plates with the sauce poured over.

Preparation and cooking time 25 minutes

Serving suggestions I like to serve this with Creamed Spinach (page 111) and tagliatelle dressed with butter, black pepper and a little chopped fresh thyme. If you only have dried thyme, then add this to the water in which you boil the pasta.

Hints and variations To save time, you can part-cook the beef in advance. Simply brown the meat and follow the instructions up to the end of Step 4, but do not keep the meat warm. When you are ready to serve, replace the meat and finish the recipe.

Photograph opposite:
Moroccan-style Quail with Saffron and Sultana Sauce (see page 42)

Fillet steaks with creamy mushrooms and tarragon

This sauce is quite rich, so keep your vegetable accompaniments simple to set it off. Colour is important in presentation, so go for a contrast of white potatoes, green broccoli and orange carrots, for example.

SERVES 4

1 onion, finely chopped

60 ml/4 tbsp olive oil

175 g/6 oz mushrooms, sliced

200 ml/7 fl oz/scant 1 cup white wine

4 fillet steaks, about 175 g/6 oz each

150 ml/¼ pt/⅔ cup double (heavy) cream

1 garlic clove, crushed

30 ml/2 tbsp fresh tarragon, chopped OR 10 ml/2 tsp dried tarragon

10 ml/2 tsp French mustard

Salt and freshly ground black pepper

TO GARNISH
Sprigs of fresh tarragon

1 Fry (sauté) the onion in half the oil until softened but not browned. Add the mushrooms and cook for a further 2 minutes. Add the wine and simmer for 5 minutes.

2 Meanwhile, flatten the steaks with a rolling pin and sear on both sides in another pan in the remaining oil. Cook for 4–12 minutes, depending on how well you like them cooked.

3 Stir the cream, garlic, tarragon and mustard into the onion and mushroom mixture and heat gently for 4–5 minutes. Season with salt and pepper.

4 Pour the sauce on to warm plates and set the steaks on top. Garnish with tarragon.

Preparation and cooking time 25–35 minutes

Serving suggestions New potatoes and plain fresh vegetables will complement the richness of the dish perfectly.

Old-fashioned beef casserole with mustard

This is a comforting all-in-one meal that needs very little attention once it's assembled – just leave it to cook slowly in the oven. That's ideal if you want to return home to a hot meal after a day's skiing or a brisk country walk.

SERVES 6

300 ml/¹/₂ pt/1¹/₄ cups brown ale or stout

30 ml/2 tbsp cornflour (cornstarch)

150 ml/¹/₄ pt/²/₃ cup boiling water

2 beef stock cubes

20 ml/4 tsp wholegrain mustard

30 g/1 oz/2 tbsp butter or margarine

6 potatoes, sliced

700 g/1¹/₂ lb braising steak, cubed

12 shallots, peeled

350 g/12 oz button mushrooms, wiped

2 garlic cloves, crushed

15 ml/1 tbsp black treacle (molasses)

2 bay leaves

15 ml/1 tbsp chopped fresh parsley

Salt and freshly ground black pepper

30 ml/2 tbsp chopped fresh thyme

1 Blend a little of the ale or stout with the cornflour, then stir into the boiling water. Stir in the remaining ale or stout, the stock cubes and mustard and set aside.

2 Use half of the butter or margarine to smear the base of a large casserole dish (Dutch oven) and put in about two-thirds of the sliced potatoes, reserving the rest for the topping. Add all the remaining ingredients except 15 ml/1 tbsp of the thyme and the rest of the butter or margarine.

3 Pour over the stock and ale mixture. Top with the remaining sliced potatoes, sprinkle over the reserved thyme and dot with the last of the butter or margarine.

4 Cover and cook in a preheated oven at 160°C /325°F/gas 3/fan oven 145°C for 2¹/₂ hours.

5 Remove the lid and place under a hot grill (broiler), if liked, to crisp the top – this will give the dish a lovely golden, appetising appearance.

Preparation and cooking time 2³/₄ hours

Serving suggestions If you like, you could serve a green vegetable with the casserole, but it's not really necessary, as there are so many good things in it already.

Flemish beef carbonnade with a garlic crust

The sweet taste of the carbonnade complements the garlic crust surprisingly well. As with lots of casseroles, the flavour improves if you make it in advance, then reheat it when you are ready.

SERVES 6

1.5 kg/3 lb lean braising steak, cut into wide strips

15 ml/1 tbsp olive oil

100 g/4 oz/½ cup unsalted (sweet) butter or beef dripping

3 large onions, sliced

4 garlic cloves, crushed

Salt and freshly ground black pepper

30 ml/2 tbsp plain (all-purpose) flour

15 ml/1 tbsp soft brown sugar

300 ml/½ pt/1¼ cups strong beef stock

450 ml/¾ pt/2 cups brown ale

15 ml/1 tbsp red wine vinegar

1 bouquet garni

2 bay leaves

FOR THE GARLIC CRUST
225 g/8 oz/1 cup unsalted (sweet) butter

3 garlic cloves

1 French stick, cut into 2.5 cm/1 in thick slices

1 Brown the beef quickly in the oil and butter or dripping. Lift the meat out of the pan and put aside.

2 Cook the onions in the hot fat until golden, then add the garlic and cook for 1–2 minutes, then lift out with a draining spoon. Starting with the onions, layer the onions and beef in a deep casserole dish (Dutch oven), lightly seasoning each layer with salt and pepper.

3 To the pan juices, add the flour and sugar and cook for 1 minute, stirring. Stir in a little of the stock until the mixture is smooth. Bring to the boil and add the remaining stock, the ale and vinegar. Bring the mixture to the boil again. Put the bouquet garni and bay leaves into the casserole, pour the sauce over the meat and cook in a preheated oven at 160°C/325°F/gas 3/fan oven 145°C for 2½ hours.

4 For the garlic crust, melt the butter in a frying pan (skillet) and add the garlic. Dip the bread slices in the garlic butter to soak one side.

5 Put the bread on top of the casserole, buttered side up. Return to the oven, uncovered, for a further 15 minutes or until the garlic crust is golden.

6 Serve straight from the cooking dish.

Preparation and cooking time 3¼ hours

Serving suggestions Steamed Cauliflower with Almonds (page 99) and Turkish Fried Carrots (page 98) will add lots of colour and texture to the meal.

Hints and variations If making in advance, prepare up to the end of Step 3, then chill. Reheat thoroughly **before** continuing from Step 4 and always make sure it is piping hot before serving.

Spiced beef casserole with orange and rum

*The combination of rich and tangy flavours in this warm, aromatic casserole will
provide a wonderful welcome to your guests at the end of a cold day on the slopes –
or in the winter rain!*

SERVES 4

750 g/1¾ lb stewing beef, cubed

175 g/6 oz button mushrooms

30 ml/2 tbsp sunflower oil

40 g/1½ oz/3 tbsp plain
(all-purpose) flour

300 ml/½ pt/1¼ cups beef stock

300 ml/½ pt/1¼ cups orange juice

10 ml/2 tsp white wine vinegar

10 ml/2 tsp soft brown sugar

2.5 ml/½ tsp ground cinnamon

1 bouquet garni

Grated zest of ½ orange

15 ml/1 tbsp rum

Salt and freshly ground black pepper

1 Fry (sauté) the meat and mushrooms in the oil in an ovenproof
casserole dish (Dutch oven) until browned. Stir in the flour and cook
for 1 minute.

2 Blend in the stock and orange juice and stir in the remaining
ingredients. Bring to the boil, cover and cook in a preheated oven at
180°C/350°F/gas 4/fan oven 160°C for 2½ hours.

3 Remove the bouquet garni, taste and re-season before serving.

Preparation and cooking time 2¾ hours

Serving suggestions Potato Patties (page 108) and Fried Peas with
Garlic (page 101) make good accompaniments.

Greek-style beef with feta

This traditional Greek recipe is often made using rabbit instead of beef and, although rabbit is not all that popular now, it does make a lovely dish. It is ideal for cooking in a slo-cooker – it will take about 6 hours.

SERVES 6

1 kg/2¼ lb lean braising steak or shin of beef, cut into 2 cm/¾ in cubes

50 g/2 oz/½ cup seasoned plain (all-purpose) flour

75 ml/5 tbsp sunflower oil

1.5 ml/¼ tsp cumin seeds

5 cm/2 in piece of cinnamon stick

45 ml/3 tbsp tomato purée (paste)

30 ml/2 tbsp herb vinegar

Salt and freshly ground black pepper

900 ml/1½ pts/3¾ cups beef stock

2 sprigs of fresh thyme

4 small onions, peeled

100 g/4 oz/1 cup feta cheese, cubed

TO GARNISH
Sprigs of fresh thyme

1 Toss the meat in the seasoned flour. Fry (sauté) in the oil and transfer to a casserole dish (Dutch oven).

2 Add the cumin seeds, cinnamon stick and tomato purée to the juices remaining in the pan. Stir in the vinegar, salt and pepper, stock and thyme. Bring to the boil and pour over the meat.

3 Cover and cook in a preheated oven at 160°C/325°F/gas 3/fan oven 145°C for 2½ hours.

4 Plunge the onions into boiling water, drain and add to the casserole and cook for a further 30 minutes.

5 Add the cubed cheese and return to the oven until the cheese begins to melt.

6 Garnish with fresh thyme before serving.

Preparation and cooking time 3¼ hours

Serving suggestions To complete your Greek-style meal, serve with plain rice, pitta breads and salad.

Hints and variations If you can't get feta, a crumbly white cheese like Cheshire or Wensleydale will do quite well.

Italian lamb with Parma ham and pesto

This uses one of my favourite cooking methods – everything ends up in the same pan! It's so easy but really tasty. It's also a great combination of Italian flavours, mixing the lamb, Parma ham and pesto.

SERVES 4

750 g/1¾ lb lamb fillet, cut into medallions 5 mm/¼ in thick

30 ml/2 tbsp seasoned plain (all-purpose) flour

45 ml/3 tbsp olive oil

25 g/1 oz/2 tbsp butter or margarine

1 garlic clove, crushed

100 g/4 oz button mushrooms, sliced

75 g/3 oz/¾ cup Parma ham, cut into thin strips

10 ml/2 tsp pesto

45 ml/3 tbsp freshly grated Parmesan cheese

1 Flatten the lamb medallions slightly with a meat mallet or rolling pin and dust with the seasoned flour.

2 Quickly fry (sauté) in half the oil and butter or margarine, turning once. Remove the lamb and keep warm.

3 Using the fat remaining in the pan, fry the garlic and mushrooms for 3 minutes, then add the ham and pesto and cook for a further minute.

4 Return the lamb to the pan and, stirring everything together, cook for a further 2 minutes.

5 Transfer to warm plates and sprinkle with the Parmesan before serving.

Preparation and cooking time 20 minutes

Serving suggestions I like to serve this with simple accompaniments such as pasta tossed in butter and black pepper and a green salad.

Roast rack of lamb with orange and port sauce

Ask the butcher to 'French-trim' the racks of lamb for you. This means removing all visible fat and scraping the ends of the bones clean. You can buy miniature paper chefs' hats to sit on the ends of the bones if you wish! See central cover photograph.

SERVES 4

2 x 350 g/12 oz racks of lamb, French-trimmed

15 ml/1 tbsp olive oil

15 ml/1 tbsp plain (all-purpose) flour

15 ml/1 tbsp redcurrant jelly (clear conserve)

120 ml/4 fl oz/½ cup fresh orange juice

200 ml/7 fl oz/scant 1 cup vegetable stock

5 ml/1 tsp dark soy sauce

30 ml/2 tbsp port

TO GARNISH
A few fresh sage leaves

1 Score the skin of the lamb in a diagonal fashion, place in a roasting tin (pan) and brush with a little oil.

2 Roast in a preheated oven at 220°C/425°F/gas 7/fan oven 200°C for 20 minutes. The lamb should still be slightly pink inside; add another 5 minutes if you prefer it well done.

3 Once cooked, remove the lamb from the roasting tin, cover with foil and keep warm. Set the roasting tin on the hob on a medium heat and stir the flour into the oil to make a smooth paste.

4 Stir in the redcurrant jelly, orange juice and stock and then bring to the boil, stirring all the time. Cook for about 3 minutes until thickened and smooth. Stir in the soy sauce and port.

5 Cut the rack into cutlets and transfer to warm plates. Garnish with the sage leaves and serve with the sauce.

Preparation and cooking time 35–40 minutes

Serving suggestions The cutlets go very well with my Potato Patties (page 108). Put one potato patty on each warmed plate. Cut each rack into six cutlets and arrange three on each potato patty. Pour the sauce around and serve with a green vegetable.

Marinated roast lamb with lemon and herbs

If you have any leftovers – which is, I have to say, unlikely! – they are delicious eaten cold the next day. Try to use fresh herbs as the flavour really is superior. They are easy to buy in the supermarket – or grow in the window box.

SERVES 6

2.25 kg/5 lb leg of lamb, boned

75 ml/5 tbsp chopped fresh thyme OR 25 ml/5 tsp dried

75 ml/5 tbsp chopped fresh rosemary OR 15 ml/1 tbsp dried

15 ml/1 tbsp sea salt

45 ml/3 tbsp coarsely crushed black peppercorns

Juice of 2 lemons

200 ml/7 fl oz/scant 1 cup olive oil

100 ml/3½ fl oz/scant ½ cup balsamic vinegar

Salt and freshly ground black pepper

TO GARNISH
1 lemon, cut into wedges

1 Lay the meat flat on a work surface and beat with a rolling pin. Slash through the thickest parts of the muscle (this will help the marinade and heat to penetrate evenly).

2 Mix the herbs with the seasoning in a bowl. Rub this mixture into the cut side of the meat.

3 Place the meat in a shallow dish. Mix together the lemon juice, olive oil and balsamic vinegar. Pour the mixture over the meat. Leave to marinate for 1½ hours, turning once or twice.

4 Preheat the grill (broiler) to high.

5 Remove the meat from the marinade, pat dry with kitchen paper (paper towels) and season with salt and pepper.

6 Grill (broil) for 2–3 minutes on high, then turn and grill the other side for 2–3 minutes. Lower the heat and grill for 15–18 minutes more, turning once.

7 Leave to rest for 5–10 minutes, then cut into slices.

8 Garnish with the wedges of lemon before serving.

Preparation and cooking time 40–50 minutes plus marinating

Serving suggestions I like to serve the sliced lamb on a large platter, garnished with the wedges of lemon, accompanied by Salsa Verde (page 48). French (green) beans make a good side dish.

Roasted soy lamb fillets in a lime and garlic marinade

Although the cooking time here is short, you must allow time in advance for marinating as the marinade actually tenderises and starts almost to 'cook' the meat. If you have a busy day, this is best done overnight.

SERVES 4

2 x lamb neck fillets, about 350 g/12 oz each

FOR THE MARINADE
Juice of 1 lime

30 ml/2 tbsp soy sauce

15 ml/1 tbsp olive oil

1 garlic clove, crushed

1 Trim the lamb of fat and sinew. Mix the marinade ingredients together and pour over the lamb. Leave to marinate for at least 12 hours.

2 Remove the lamb from its marinade and roast on a rack in a preheated oven at 230°C/450°F/gas 8/fan oven 210°C for 20–25 minutes, depending on how well done you like your meat.

3 Leave to rest for about 5 minutes before slicing and serving.

Preparation and cooking time 30–35 minutes plus marinating

Serving suggestions Cut the lamb into thin slices and arrange on a large serving platter. I like to accompany this dish with Orange-glazed Turnips (page 112) and Classic Potatoes with Cream (page 106).

Hints and variations Boned loin makes a delicious, if rather expensive, alternative to the neck fillets.

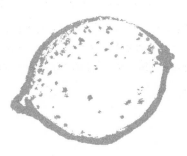

Shortcut Shrewsbury lamb

The preparation and cooking in this recipe are much quicker than the traditional method, yet none of the delicious flavour is lost. If you fancy a change, try it with different types of mushrooms.

SERVES 4

25 g/1 oz/2 tbsp butter or margarine

8 lamb cutlets

100 g/4 oz button mushrooms, sliced

200 ml/7 fl oz/scant 1 cup stock

60 ml/4 tbsp redcurrant jelly (clear conserve)

Juice of ½ lemon

30 ml/2 tbsp Worcestershire sauce

A little freshly grated nutmeg

Salt and freshly ground black pepper

1 Heat the butter or margarine in a frying pan (skillet) and seal the cutlets on both sides.

2 Put the cutlets into an ovenproof dish.

3 Gently fry (sauté) the mushrooms in the frying pan until softened, then spoon them over the lamb cutlets.

4 Add the stock to the frying pan and boil rapidly to reduce by half, then add the redcurrant jelly, lemon juice and Worcestershire sauce. Season with the nutmeg, salt and pepper.

5 Pour the sauce over the lamb and cook in a preheated oven at 180°C/350°F/gas 4/fan oven 160°C for about 20 minutes, depending on how well you like your lamb cooked.

6 Transfer the lamb to warmed plates and spoon the sauce over.

Preparation and cooking time 30–35 minutes

Serving suggestions Serve with a good helping of creamy mashed potatoes and Steamed Broccoli with Garlic and Mustard Seeds (page 97).

Tagine barrogog bis basela

This is a North African lamb stew, absolutely delicious but very rich. The honey's sweetness is countered by the black pepper and spices. The name itself can be quite a dinner-party talking point!

SERVES 8

1 kg/2¼ lb boned shoulder, leg or neck fillet of lamb, cut into large pieces

Salt

10 ml/2 tsp freshly ground black pepper

2.5 ml/½ tsp saffron powder or ground turmeric

5 ml/1 tsp ground ginger

2 garlic cloves, crushed

1 large onion, grated

1 small bunch of fresh parsley, finely chopped

60 ml/4 tbsp olive oil

450 g/1 lb/2⅔ cups prunes, stoned (pitted) and chopped

10 ml/2 tsp ground cinnamon

15–60 ml/1–4 tbsp clear honey

45 ml/3 tbsp orange flower water

TO GARNISH
Blanched almonds, chopped

1 Put the lamb in a saucepan with a little salt, the pepper, saffron or turmeric, ginger, garlic, onion, parsley and 45 ml/3 tbsp of the oil. Add enough water to cover and simmer, covered, for 1½ hours or until the meat is very tender.

2 Add the prunes and cinnamon and cook for a further 15 minutes.

3 Sweeten to taste with honey, add the orange water and cook for a few more minutes until the sauce is quite thick.

4 When ready to serve, transfer the meat to warm plates. Fry (sauté) the almonds in the remaining oil and sprinkle over the meat.

Preparation and cooking time About 2 hours

Serving suggestions Serve with lots of French bread to mop up those fragrant juices. A tomato salad makes a refreshing side dish.

Hints and variations The cooking time is long, but you could prepare and cook it in advance, then reheat when required.

Roast leg of lamb with red wine and ginger

Another delectable variation on a simple roast, this won't spoil once cooked, so you simply cover it with foil and keep it warm in a very low oven while you enjoy some time with your guests.

SERVES ABOUT 8

2 kg/4½ lb leg of lamb

2 garlic cloves, cut into slivers

A few small sprigs of fresh rosemary

15 ml/1 tbsp olive oil

Salt and freshly ground black pepper

10 ml/2 tsp ground ginger

50 g/2 oz/¼ cup unsalted (sweet) butter

2 onions, sliced

2 carrots, chopped

4 sprigs of fresh thyme

300 ml/½ pt/1¼ cups red wine

30 ml/2 tbsp redcurrant jelly (clear conserve)

1 Pierce the lamb with the point of a sharp knife and push garlic slivers and rosemary into these holes.

2 Rub the skin with the oil, a little salt and pepper and the ginger.

3 Melt the butter in a roasting tin (pan) and quickly brown the lamb all over. Remove from the tin, add the onions and carrots and fry (sauté) until golden brown. Put the sprigs of thyme on top of the vegetables and the meat on top. Cover with foil.

4 Roast in a preheated oven at 220°C/425°F/gas 7/fan oven 200°C for 25 minutes.

5 Pour the wine over, reduce the heat to 180°C/350°F/gas 4/fan oven 160°C and cook for a further 1¼ hours, basting 2–3 times.

6 Remove the joint from the tin, then strain the cooking juices and add the redcurrant jelly. Boil until reduced by a third. Remove any fat from the juices and season with salt and pepper if necessary.

7 Slice the lamb and arrange on plates or a large platter. Pour the sauce into a sauceboat and serve with the lamb.

Preparation and cooking time about 2¼ hours

Serving suggestions I like to accompany this with Creamy Courgette Bake (page 100), roast potatoes and carrots.

seafood main courses

Fish and seafood cook in just a few minutes so they make superb, light main courses, especially if you are looking for something quick. Some people don't like fiddling with bones, though, so don't go for whole fish if you are not sure. You can buy 'lazy' root ginger, ready chopped, in jars from your supermarket. I find it a great standby for many fish dishes.

Gingered prawns with stir-fried broccoli

*I love the lightness of this recipe. For chalet parties, I often serve it with noodles
instead of the brown rice, which makes it into a more substantial dish and therefore
more suitable for appetites sharpened by a day on the pistes.*

SERVES 2

**250 g/9 oz cooked peeled
prawns (shrimp)**

**2.5 cm/1 in piece of fresh root ginger,
peeled and finely chopped
OR 5 ml/1 tsp 'lazy' ginger**

15 ml/1 tbsp medium or dry sherry

1 egg white

5 ml/1 tsp cornflour (cornstarch)

45 ml/3 tbsp sunflower oil

**FOR THE STIR-FRIED BROCCOLI
2 spring onions (scallions),
finely chopped**

**250 g/9 oz broccoli,
divided into small florets**

2.5 ml/½ tsp salt

5 ml/1 tsp caster (superfine) sugar

1 Put the prawns into a bowl with the ginger, sherry, egg white and
cornflour. Stir well and leave in the fridge to marinate for at least
20 minutes.

2 Heat 15 ml/1 tbsp of the oil in a wok and add the prawns. Stir-fry
over moderate heat for about 30 seconds. Remove from the wok
with a draining spoon and set aside while you make the stir-fried
broccoli.

3 Heat the remaining oil in the wok. Add the spring onions and
broccoli and stir well. Add the salt and sugar and stir-fry until the
broccoli is just tender. Return the prawns to the wok and stir to mix
with the broccoli.

4 Serve immediately.

Preparation and cooking time 15 minutes plus marinating

Serving suggestions I think this is delicious served on a bed of nutty
brown rice.

Pescada a la marina

This is one of my favourite ways of serving fish and has always proved popular with adults and children alike. In the unlikely event of there being any leftovers, they taste equally good served cold the following day.

SERVES 6

700 g/1½ lb haddock or cod fillets, cut into strips

60 ml/4 tbsp olive oil

30 ml/2 tbsp lemon juice

1 small onion, finely chopped

1 garlic clove, crushed

2 bay leaves

5 ml/1 tsp salt

Freshly ground black pepper

A pinch of freshly grated nutmeg

1 egg, lightly beaten

100 g/4 oz/2 cups fresh breadcrumbs

A little sunflower oil, for cooking

1 Put the fish into a shallow dish. Blend together the olive oil, lemon juice, onion, garlic and bay leaves and add the salt and pepper and nutmeg to taste. Pour over the fish and leave to marinate for at least 1 hour, turning from time to time.

2 Dry the fish on kitchen paper (paper towels), dip in the beaten egg, then the breadcrumbs. Leave to dry and harden a little (this will take 10–15 minutes).

3 Fry (sauté) the fish on both sides in hot oil and drain on kitchen paper.

4 Serve hot or cold.

Preparation and cooking time 15–20 minutes plus marinating

Serving suggestions For a hot meal, Lemon Potatoes (page 105) make a good accompaniment. A green salad will finish off the dish, whether the fillets are served hot or cold.

Glazed salmon with hoisin and ginger

Serve these salmon fillets cut into two or three pieces on a bed of freshly cooked pasta so that you can see the contrast of the lovely pink fish and the golden effect of the glaze. It's really quick and easy to make.

SERVES 4

30 ml/2 tbsp hoisin sauce

30 ml/2 tbsp dark soy sauce

5 ml/1 tsp sesame oil

10 ml/2 tsp clear honey

1 garlic clove, crushed

5 ml/1 tsp grated fresh root ginger

4 salmon steaks, about 150 g/5 oz each

1 Place all the ingredients except the salmon in a small mixing bowl and stir until well combined.

2 Brush each salmon steak with the glaze and grill (broil) for 3–4 minutes on each side, basting with any remaining glaze, until golden and cooked through.

3 Serve immediately.

Preparation and cooking time 10–15 minutes

Serving suggestions Plain pasta with a spoonful of pesto stirred into it makes a colourful accompaniment, and a mixed salad will provide further contrast of texture. Alternatively, you could offer a green vegetable, such as French (green) beans.

Herb-crusted salmon with rich tomato sauce

Salmon is a substantial fish and so can easily take on the full flavours of this rich tomato sauce, which also adds good colour to the dish. You can also use salmon steaks for this recipe.

SERVES 4

3–4 slices of ciabatta or white bread

25 g/1 oz black olives, pitted (stoned)

15 g/½ oz anchovy fillets

2 small shallots or ½ onion

2 small whole garlic cloves

30 ml/2 tbsp chopped fresh basil

15 ml/1 tbsp olive oil

Salt and freshly ground black pepper

4 skinless salmon fillets, about 150 g/5 oz each

65 g/2½ oz/scant ⅓ cup butter or margarine, melted

450 g/1 lb ripe tomatoes, halved and seeded

2.5 ml/½ tsp caster (superfine) sugar

1 Roughly chop the bread, olives, anchovies and shallots or onion. Place in a food processor with 1 garlic clove, 15 ml/1 tbsp of the basil and the olive oil, and season with salt and pepper.

2 Brush the salmon steaks with a little of the melted butter or margarine and press the crumbs on to each fillet.

3 Liquidise the tomatoes until smooth and then push through a sieve (strainer). Stir in the remaining whole garlic clove, the remaining basil and the sugar. Taste and adjust the seasoning if necessary. Cover and leave to marinate for at least 15 minutes.

4 Place the salmon in a small roasting tin (pan) with the remaining melted butter or margarine poured over. Cook in a preheated oven at 200°C/400°F/gas 6/fan oven 180°C for 10–15 minutes.

5 Meanwhile, gently warm the tomato sauce without boiling.

6 Remove the salmon from the oven and strain the juices into the tomato sauce, removing the whole garlic clove. Taste and adjust the seasoning if necessary.

7 Serve the fish on warm plates with the sauce poured over.

Preparation and cooking time 30 minutes plus marinating

Serving suggestions I like to serve this with Potato Stacks (page 109) and Stir-fried Broccoli (page 63).

Sautéed trout fillets with lemon butter sauce

This works just as well with whole fish, but I prefer to use fillets as they're less fiddly to eat. Before you cook them for guests, just check the fish over and remove any stray bones with tweezers.

SERVES 4

4 large trout fillets

2.5 ml/½ tsp dried rosemary

2.5 ml/½ tsp salt

1.5 ml/¼ tsp freshly ground black pepper

25 g/1 oz/¼ cup plain (all-purpose) flour

120 ml/4 fl oz/½ cup sunflower oil

50 g/2 oz/¼ cup butter or margarine

Juice of 1 lemon

30 ml/2 tbsp chopped fresh parsley

1 Sprinkle the fish with the rosemary, salt and pepper and coat with flour.

2 Fry (sauté) the fish in the oil for 4–5 minutes on each side, until just cooked. Remove the fish and keep warm.

3 Pour off the oil, then add the butter or margarine, lemon juice and parsley to the pan and cook for about 1 minute, stirring any residue from the bottom of the pan to give a well-flavoured sauce.

4 Transfer the fillets to a large platter or individual plates. Pour over the sauce and serve.

Preparation and cooking time 10–15 minutes

Serving suggestions The lemony juices combine well with boiled potatoes, French Beans with Onion and Garlic (page 95) and sweetcorn (corn).

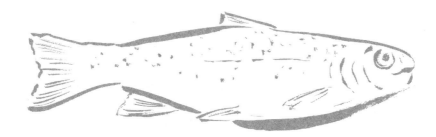

Fillets of trout in Pernod sauce

Don't be tempted to add more Pernod than I've suggested. This sauce just needs a hint of it to match the mushrooms and cream. More would kill the trout's delicate flavour and destroy the balance of the sauce.

SERVES 4

4 large trout fillets

30 ml/2 tbsp seasoned plain (all-purpose) flour

100 g/4 oz/½ cup unsalted (sweet) butter

225 g/8 oz button mushrooms, thinly sliced

1 garlic clove, crushed

45 ml/3 tbsp Pernod

150 ml/¼ pt/⅔ cup double (heavy) cream

Salt and freshly ground black pepper

1 Coat the trout fillets in seasoned flour and fry (sauté) in the butter for 4–5 minutes on each side. Transfer to a serving dish and keep warm.

2 Fry the mushrooms and garlic in the trout juices over a gentle heat for 3–4 minutes.

3 Stir in the Pernod and simmer for 3–4 minutes.

4 Add the cream, season with salt and pepper and heat gently.

5 Serve the trout on warm plates with the sauce poured over.

Preparation and cooking time 25 minutes

Serving suggestions For a quick, simple and delicious meal, serve with baked potatoes and a crisp green salad.

Crisp whiting fillets with orange and parsley butter

Lemon is the usual citrus accompaniment to fish recipes, but for this recipe I have used orange, imparting a delicate and less strident flavour. My guests' reactions prove it was a good choice.

SERVES 4

4 fresh whiting fillets, approximately 150 g/5 oz each, skinned and boned

30 ml/2 tbsp seasoned plain (all-purpose) flour

50 g/2 oz/¼ cup unsalted (sweet) butter

30 ml/2 tbsp chopped fresh parsley

5 ml/1 tsp grated orange zest

Salt and freshly ground black pepper

TO GARNISH
Sprigs of watercress

1 Coat the fish lightly in the seasoned flour.

2 Blend the butter with the parsley and orange zest and season to taste with salt and pepper.

3 Heat the butter mix in a frying pan (skillet), add the whiting fillets and cook for 4–5 minutes on each side, until golden and cooked through.

4 Garnish with watercress before serving.

Preparation and cooking time 15–20 minutes

Serving suggestions Sautéed sweet potatoes make an unusual accompaniment for this dish. I also like to offer some brown bread and butter.

Hints and variations You can use any firm-fleshed white fish for this recipe.

Feuilletés de St Jacques

Scallops are amazingly versatile and are suitable for grilling, frying, poaching and baking. In this recipe they are combined with creamy leeks and served in a light puff pastry case – simply divine.

SERVES 4

1 sheet of ready-rolled puff pastry (paste)

1 egg yolk

2 small leeks, finely sliced

A pinch of caster (superfine) sugar

45 ml/3 tbsp crème fraîche

Salt and freshly ground black pepper

1 lime

12 frozen scallops

50 g/2 oz/¼ cup butter or margarine

TO GARNISH
Sprigs of fresh chervil

1 Cut the puff pastry into four rectangles. With a sharp knife, lightly score a rectangle about 1 cm/½ in inside each one, without cutting right through the pastry. Brush with the egg yolk.

2 Bake in a preheated oven at 190°C/375°F/gas 5/fan oven 170°C for about 20 minutes, or until golden brown.

3 When the pastry is cooked, lift the central rectangle out of each piece of pastry. These will form the lids and the cavities you have made will house the filling.

4 Meanwhile, put the leeks in a saucepan with the sugar and crème fraîche. Season with salt and pepper and add a squeeze of lime juice.

5 Cook for 10 minutes on a medium heat. You may need to add a little more crème fraîche if it starts to dry up, so keep an eye on the mixture.

6 Cut each scallop into three pieces, add to the leeks and cook for 5 minutes.

7 Add the butter or margarine and stir until melted.

8 Using a slotted spoon and leaving the liquids in the pan, lift the leeks and scallops into the pastry cases (pie shells), dividing the mixture evenly.

9 Boil the liquids rapidly to reduce to a sauce and pour over the scallops and leeks in their cases. Decorate with the chervil, then put the lids on and serve immediately.

Preparation and cooking time 35 minutes

Serving suggestions A dish of freshly cooked sautéed potatoes and a tomato salad will complete your meal perfectly.

Heavenly fish bake with golden potato topping

This recipe is a cross between a pie and a casserole. It contains rather more prawns than cod, giving it a really sophisticated taste and appearance. You could alter the balance or use other white fish if you prefer.

SERVES 6

6 cod steaks, about 100 g/4 oz each

450 ml/³/₄ pt/2 cups milk

6 whole black peppercorns

2 bay leaves

2 leeks, thinly sliced

50 g/2 oz/¹/₄ cup unsalted (sweet) butter

25 g/1 oz/¹/₄ cup plain (all-purpose) flour

250 ml/8 fl oz/1 cup white wine

10 ml/2 tsp dried dill (dill weed)

5 ml/1 tsp dill seed

25 ml/1¹/₂ tbsp lemon juice

Salt and freshly ground black pepper

450 g/1 lb cooked peeled prawns (shrimp)

4 tomatoes, chopped

750 g/1³/₄ lb potatoes, cooked and thinly sliced

30 ml/2 tbsp olive oil

30 ml/2 tbsp freshly grated Parmesan cheese

1 Put the cod, milk, peppercorns and bay leaves into a saucepan. Bring to the boil, then reduce the heat and simmer for 6–7 minutes.

2 Remove the fish and break into biggish flakes before putting into an ovenproof dish. Strain the milk and set aside.

3 Fry (sauté) the leeks gently in the butter for 5 minutes. Stir in the flour and cook for 1 minute. Gradually stir in the reserved milk and the wine and cook, stirring all the time, until thickened and smooth.

4 Remove from the heat and add the dill, dill seed and lemon juice. Season with salt and pepper.

5 Arrange the prawns and chopped tomatoes on top of the cod and pour the sauce over. Top with the sliced potatoes, brush them with olive oil and sprinkle with the Parmesan cheese.

6 Cook in a preheated oven at 190°C/375°F/gas 5/fan oven 170°C for about 30 minutes until the topping is golden brown.

Preparation and cooking time 45 minutes

Serving suggestions I like to serve this with a large dish of colourful roasted vegetables and Garlic Rosti (page 109).

Fruits de mer en papillote

These little seafood parcels are best opened at the table, so that your guests can appreciate the delicious aroma as it is released. You can use foil for the parcels if you don't have any baking parchment. See photograph opposite page 96.

SERVES 4

4 leeks, thinly sliced

4 cod fillets, about 100 g/4 oz each

100 g/4 oz cooked peeled prawns (shrimp)

30 ml/2 tbsp dill (dill weed), roughly chopped

Salt and freshly ground black pepper

25 g/1 oz/2 tbsp unsalted (sweet) butter, melted

Juice of 1 lemon

TO GARNISH
Slices of lemon

1 Cut four circles of baking parchment, about 30 cm/12 in in diameter. Fold in half, then open out again.

2 Scatter the sliced leeks over half of each circle and top with the cod. Divide the prawns equally among the parcels, sprinkle over the dill and season with salt and pepper. Pour on the melted butter and lemon juice.

3 Fold the paper over each parcel and roll the edges tightly together. Place on a baking (cookie) sheet and cook in a preheated oven at 200°C/400°F/gas 6/fan oven 180°C for 10–15 minutes.

4 Put each parcel on a warm plate and garnish with the lemon.

Preparation and cooking time 25–30 minutes

Serving suggestions These go well with new potatoes, but I often serve them with rice and a side dish of Baby Carrots with Orange and Cardamom (page 98).

Hints and variations The parcels take up quite a bit of space in the oven – something to think about when deciding what vegetables to serve with them.

Thai grilled fish with lime

This light and delicious recipe is suitable for any kind of thin white fish. It couldn't be simpler to prepare but is absolutely delicious. You will need to be careful when transferring the cooked fillets to the plates as they will be very delicate.

SERVES 4

4 plaice fillets, skinned

5 ml/1 tsp salt

Juice of 2 limes

90 ml/6 tbsp soft brown sugar

1 Sprinkle the fillets with the salt and lime juice and leave to marinate for 20–25 minutes.

2 Sprinkle the sugar over and grill (broil) for about 5 minutes, without turning, until the fillets are cooked and the sugar has caramelised.

3 Serve immediately.

Preparation and cooking time 7 minutes plus marinating

Serving suggestions Arrange the fillets on a bed of buttered plain rice and serve with Garlic Carrots and Courgettes with Lime (page 99).

Marinated salmon steaks with orange and honey

Here's another recipe that takes minimal cooking, although you must set aside time for marinating. I usually leave it overnight.

SERVES 6

75 ml/5 tbsp sunflower oil

Juice and grated zest of 2 limes

45 ml/3 tbsp orange juice

5 ml/1 tsp clear honey

2 green cardamoms, crushed

6 salmon steaks, about 175 g/6 oz each

1 Mix the oil with the lime juice and zest, the orange juice, honey and cardamoms. Pour this marinade over the fish and leave for several hours, overnight if possible.

2 Drain, reserving the marinade. Grill (broil) the salmon for about 4 minutes on each side.

3 Meanwhile, bring the marinade to the boil and keep warm.

4 Serve the steaks on warm plates with the marinade poured over.

Preparation and cooking time 15 minutes plus marinating

Serving suggestions Serve with new potatoes in Anchovy Cream (page 115) and Steamed Broccoli with Garlic and Mustard Seeds (page 97) or a mixed salad.

Bacon-wrapped cod fillets with tarragon cream sauce

Weaving the bacon to make the wrapping for the fish is a bit fiddly, but once you've done the first one it's plain sailing! The little parcels hold together well during cooking and they look and taste delightful.

SERVES 4

24 rashers (slices) of streaky bacon, rinded

4 cod fillets, about 100 g/4 oz each

1 onion, finely chopped

50 g/2 oz/¼ cup unsalted (sweet) butter

150 ml/¼ pt/⅔ cup white wine

2.5 ml/½ tsp dried tarragon

60 ml/4 tbsp double (heavy) cream

1 Stretch the bacon rashers with the back of a knife.

2 Weave six of them into a square and put one of the fish portions into the centre. Fold the overlapping bacon around the fish to enclose it. Repeat with the remaining bacon and fish to make four parcels in all.

3 Fry (sauté) the onion in the butter until softened, then add the fish parcels and fry for 3 minutes, turning, until slightly browned all over. Add the wine and tarragon to the pan, bring to the boil, then cover, reduce the heat and simmer for 10 minutes.

4 Add the cream and season to taste with salt and pepper. Heat through without boiling, then serve.

Preparation and cooking time 35–40 minutes

Serving suggestions Try these with baked potatoes and French Beans with Onion and Garlic (page 95).

vegetarian main courses

Don't be afraid to go 'meatless' for a change – none of the dishes in this chapter contains meat or fish but they would all tempt even the most ardent carnivore! If, however, you are cooking for serious vegetarians, check the labels before you buy to make sure that any cheese or condiments you use are suitable – even Worcestershire sauce contains anchovies.

Sensational onion flan

The extra egg yolk and cream make this onion flan live up to its name – sensational. It is delicious served hot with potatoes and vegetables, but also great cold with a salad on the following day.

SERVES 6

225 g/8 oz shortcrust pastry (basic pie crust)

3 large onions, finely sliced

30 ml/2 tbsp butter or margarine

1 whole egg

1 egg yolk

300 ml/¹/₂ pt/1¹/₄ cups double (heavy) cream

Salt and freshly ground black pepper

2.5 ml/¹/₂ tsp freshly grated nutmeg

1 Set a flan (pie) ring on a baking (cookie) sheet. Line with the pastry and chill while preparing the filling.

2 Fry (sauté) the onions in the butter or margarine until softened.

3 Beat the egg, egg yolk and cream together and stir into the onions. Season with salt, pepper and nutmeg.

4 Pour into the flan ring and bake in a preheated oven at 200°C/400°F/ gas 6/fan oven 180°C for 30 minutes until golden and bubbling.

Preparation and cooking time 45 minutes

Serving suggestions This makes a really substantial meal served with jacket potatoes, Courgette Patties (page 101) and a tomato salad.

Hints and variations You can use Mascarpone cheese instead of cream, if you prefer.

Potato gratin with chilli

Though this makes a satisfying meal on its own, it also goes very well with grilled or roast meats. The touch of chilli paste gives the flavour just the lift you need when you come in from the cold.

SERVES 4

1 kg/2¼ lb potatoes, thinly sliced

45 ml/3 tbsp olive oil

10 ml/2 tsp chilli paste

3 garlic cloves, finely chopped

300 ml/½ pt/1¼ cups single (light) cream

Salt and freshly ground black pepper

1 Toss the potatoes in a large bowl with 30 ml/2 tbsp of the olive oil and all the other ingredients until the slices are evenly coated and the garlic and chilli are well distributed.

2 Transfer to a lightly oiled gratin dish, spreading out the slices; it is not necessary to layer it piece by piece, but try to ensure that most of the slices are lying flat. Pour over any cream remaining in the bowl and trickle the remainder of the olive oil all over the top.

3 Bake in a preheated oven at 190°C/375°F/gas 5/fan oven 170°C for 40–50 minutes, until the potatoes are tender and the top is browned and crisp. Keep an eye on the gratin and, if it looks a little dry, add more cream.

4 Flash under a hot grill (broiler) for 1–2 minutes to give a crisp, golden finish.

Preparation and cooking time About 1 hour

Serving suggestions A large loaf of warm, crusty bread and plenty of lightly cooked green beans are all you need to accompany the gratin.

Creamy mushroom risotto with thyme and lemon

The thyme and lemon are a wonderful Mediterranean-style combination that add a delicious, sharp contrast to the rich flavours of this creamy mushroom dish. Use whatever kind of mushrooms you prefer.

SERVES 4

90 ml/6 tbsp olive oil

2 shallots, finely chopped

2 garlic cloves, finely chopped

10 ml/2 tsp chopped fresh thyme

5 ml/1 tsp grated lemon zest

350 g/12 oz/1½ cups risotto (arborio) rice

150 ml/¼ pt/⅔ cup dry white wine

900 ml/1½ pts/3¾ cups hot vegetable stock

450 g/1 lb mushrooms, sliced if large

15 ml/1 tbsp chopped fresh flat-leaf parsley

Salt and freshly ground black pepper

TO DECORATE
Sprigs of fresh thyme

1 Heat half the oil in a heavy-based pan. Add the shallots, garlic, chopped thyme and lemon zest and fry (sauté) for 5 minutes or until soft. Add the rice and stir for 1 minute until all the grains are glossy.

2 Add the white wine and boil rapidly until it has evaporated.

3 Gradually add the stock to the rice, a ladleful at a time, allowing each addition to be absorbed before adding more. Continue cooking until the rice is tender. This will take about 20 minutes.

4 About 5 minutes before the rice will be ready, heat the remaining oil in a large frying pan (skillet), add the mushrooms and stir-fry over a high heat for 4–5 minutes. Stir the mushrooms and chopped parsley into the rice and season to taste with salt and pepper.

5 Decorate with sprigs of thyme before serving.

Preparation and cooking time 30 minutes

Serving suggestions This dish needs nothing more than a crisp green salad and a dish of sliced tomatoes.

Hints and variations Oyster, shiitake and ceps mushrooms all work well in this or you can buy mixed packs of exotic mushrooms in supermarkets if you prefer.

Risotto rice absorbs more liquid during the cooking process than other rices, and the result is quite creamy. By varying the amount of liquid added you can make your risotto stickier or thinner to suit your own taste. The important thing is to keep the liquid warm so that the temperature of the rice doesn't drop each time you add a ladleful.

VEGETARIAN MAIN COURSES

Aubergine rolls with basil and Mozzarella

This is the sort of recipe where the quantities don't matter. The rolls will taste delicious whatever the proportions are! It's one of my favourite standbys that I love to make when aubergines are at their best.

SERVES 4

2 large aubergines (eggplants), sliced lengthways

Olive oil

Pesto

Mozzarella cheese, grated

Fresh basil leaves, torn

Salt and freshly ground black pepper

TO GARNISH
Basil leaves

1 Drizzle the aubergine slices with olive oil and cook under a hot grill (broiler) until browned on each side.

2 Spread pesto on one side of each slice and top with grated Mozzarella cheese, then sprinkle with torn basil leaves. Season with salt and pepper, roll up the slices and secure with cocktail sticks (toothpicks).

3 Arrange the rolls on a greased baking (cookie) sheet and bake in a preheated oven at 180°C/350°F/gas 4/fan oven 160°C for 8–10 minutes.

4 Garnish with basil leaves before serving.

Preparation and cooking time 15–20 minutes

Serving suggestions Garlic Rosti (page 109) and a crisp green salad will provide a refreshing colourful accompaniment.

Hints and variations As an alternative, you can cover the finished rolls with a jar of a proprietary brand of pasta sauce before baking in the oven for 10 minutes.

Spicy chick peas with spinach and mushrooms

I have used canned chick peas in this spicy one-pan meal – it saves time and the flavour and texture are just as good as if you have gone to all the trouble of soaking and cooking them yourself. Anyway, who's to know?

SERVES 2

45 ml/3 tbsp sunflower oil

7.5 ml/1½ tsp white cumin seeds

10 ml/2 tsp chopped garlic

60 ml/4 tbsp finely chopped onion

200 g/7 oz mushrooms, chopped

200 g/7 oz/1 small can of chick peas (garbanzos)

200 g/7 oz fresh spinach leaves, washed and chopped

A handful of fresh cashew nuts (optional)

45 ml/3 tbsp chopped fresh parsley

15 ml/1 tbsp garam masala

Salt and freshly ground black pepper

1 Heat the oil in a wok until quite hot. Stir-fry the cumin seeds for 30 seconds, then add the garlic and stir-fry for 30 seconds. Stir in the onion and cook for 2–3 minutes.

2 Add the mushrooms, chick peas and spinach and cook for about 4 minutes until sizzling, moistening the spinach if necessary.

3 Stir in the cashew nuts, if using. Add the parsley and garam masala and season to taste with salt and pepper. Heat through gently, then serve at once.

Preparation and cooking time 10–12 minutes

Serving suggestions Pitta or naan breads and mango chutney make good accompaniments to this Asian-style meal.

Feta cauliflower with tomato sauce

*The cinnamon and lemon juice give this dish a very interesting Middle Eastern flavour.
The feta cheese also has a lovely, slightly salty flavour that really complements the
whole dish.*

SERVES 4

1 large cauliflower, cut into florets

3 garlic cloves, crushed

1 large onion, finely chopped

60 ml/4 tbsp olive oil

**2 x 400 g/14 oz/large cans of
chopped tomatoes**

1 bay leaf

10 ml/2 tsp dried oregano

5 cm/2 in piece of cinnamon stick

Salt and freshly ground black pepper

15 ml/1 tbsp lemon juice

**100 g/4 oz/1 cup feta
cheese, crumbled**

**100 g/4 oz/1 cup Emmental (Swiss)
cheese, grated**

1 Cook the cauliflower florets in boiling, lightly salted water until just
tender.

2 Fry (sauté) the garlic and onion in half the oil until softened, then
add the tomatoes, herbs and cinnamon stick, and season with salt
and pepper. Bring to the boil, then reduce the heat and simmer for
5 minutes. Remove the cinnamon stick and bay leaf.

3 Drain the cauliflower florets, place them in a shallow ovenproof dish
and cover with the tomato sauce.

4 Sprinkle with the lemon juice and the remaining oil and scatter the
cheeses over the surface.

5 Bake in a preheated oven at 190°C/375°F/gas 5/fan oven 170°C for
25 minutes.

Preparation and cooking time 50 minutes

Serving suggestions Antibes Potatoes (page 108) and Courgette
Patties (page 101) will turn this into a meal to satisfy the heartiest
appetites.

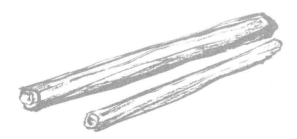

Gâteau de pommes de terre

This recipe is a prime example of how you can use the simplest ingredients to make something very sophisticated. Any potatoes will work, but my favourite variety is Maris Piper, as they seem to do everything so perfectly!

SERVES 6

500 g/18 oz potatoes

1 onion, finely chopped

15 ml/1 tbsp chopped fresh parsley

A little freshly grated nutmeg

Salt and freshly ground black pepper

225 g/8 oz puff pastry (paste)

100 ml/4 fl oz/½ cup crème fraîche

1 egg yolk

1 Slice the potatoes finely, in a food processor or on a mandolin. Dry the slices with kitchen paper (paper towels) and put them in a large bowl with the chopped onion and parsley. Season with nutmeg, salt and pepper and mix everything well.

2 Roll out the pastry and cut two rounds, each about 30 cm/12 in in diameter. Use one round to line a 30 cm/12 in flan dish (pie pan).

3 Spoon in the potato mixture and top with the crème fraîche. Put the second round of pastry on top to form a lid and seal the edges.

4 Glaze the top with the egg yolk, then make a few small holes in the centre of the lid to let the steam out during cooking.

5 Cook in a preheated oven at 180°C/350°F/gas 4/fan oven 160°C for 15 minutes, then cover lightly with foil and continue cooking for another 45 minutes.

Preparation and cooking time About 1¼ hours

Serving suggestions I like to serve this with Braised Leeks in Vermouth (page 104) and French Beans with Feta and Sun-dried Tomatoes (page 96).

Risotto bake with leeks and fresh herbs

This is even more delicious when topped with extra crème fraîche and some freshly grated Parmesan cheese. A block of Parmesan keeps well in the fridge and tastes much better than the ready-grated variety.

SERVES 8

450 g/1 lb leeks, thinly sliced

15 ml/1 tbsp olive oil

50 g/2 oz/¼ cup butter or margarine

1 onion, finely chopped

1 garlic clove, crushed

225 g/8 oz/1 cup risotto (arborio) rice

150 ml/¼ pt/⅔ cup white wine

450 ml/¾ pt/2 cups hot vegetable stock

2 eggs, lightly beaten

50 ml/2 fl oz/¼ cup crème fraîche

30 ml/2 tbsp chopped fresh parsley

15 ml/1 tbsp chopped fresh sage

1.5 ml/¼ tsp freshly grated nutmeg

50 g/2 oz/½ cup freshly grated Parmesan cheese

Salt and freshly ground black pepper

1 Fry (sauté) the leeks gently in the oil for 10 minutes and set aside.

2 Reserve 15 g/½ oz/1 tbsp of the butter or margarine. Heat the remainder and fry the onion and garlic for 3 minutes, then stir in the rice and cook for 1 minute. When the rice is transparent, stir in the wine and simmer until it is absorbed.

3 Add about a quarter of the stock and cook until this is absorbed. Repeat until all the stock has been added (this should take about 20–25 minutes).

4 Stir in the leeks.

5 Mix together the eggs, crème fraîche, parsley, sage, nutmeg and most of the Parmesan. Stir this into the rice and season with salt and pepper. Turn into a greased and lined flan dish (pie pan), sprinkle with the remaining cheese and dot the remaining butter or margarine over the surface.

6 Bake in a preheated oven at 200°C/400°F/gas 6/fan oven 180°C for 25 minutes until set and golden brown.

Preparation and cooking time About 1¼ hours

Serving suggestions For a complete vegetarian meal, I like to serve this with steamed cauliflower and Baby Carrots with Orange and Cardamom (page 98). As an alternative, you could offer a tomato sauce (see page 85).

Aubergine stacks with ratatouille

This dish contains a wonderful variety of Mediterranean vegetables, set off perfectly by the spicy harissa – a delicious North African spicy paste – and the rich flavours of the wine and cheese.

SERVES 2

1 aubergine (eggplant)

Salt and freshly ground black pepper

FOR THE RATATOUILLE
A little olive oil

1 courgette (zucchini), chopped

½ red (bell) pepper, diced

½ green pepper, diced

1 small onion, sliced

1 garlic clove, finely chopped

225 g/8 oz/1 small can of tomatoes

5 ml/1 tsp harissa paste

10 ml/2 tsp tomato purée (paste)

A splash of white wine

50 g/2 oz/⅓ packet of Boursin cheese, flavoured with garlic and herbs

60 ml/4 tbsp freshly grated Parmesan cheese

1 Thinly slice the aubergine lengthways, discarding the ends. Rub both sides of each slice with olive oil and season with lots of salt and a little pepper.

2 Place on a baking (cookie) sheet and bake in a preheated oven at 200°C/400°F/gas 6/fan oven 180°C for about 30 minutes until golden and softened.

3 Meanwhile, heat a little olive oil in a pan and add the courgette, peppers, onion and garlic and fry (sauté) for a few minutes until soft.

4 Stir in the canned tomatoes, harissa paste, tomato purée and white wine. Add the cheese and cook for about 20 minutes until tender.

5 In a flameproof dish, layer the slices of cooked aubergine and two-thirds of the ratatouille filling, finishing with sliced aubergine. Sprinkle the top of the stack generously with the Parmesan cheese, then grill (broil) until golden.

6 Serve on warm plates with the remaining filling on the side.

Preparation and cooking time 40 minutes

Serving suggestions Classic Potatoes with Cream (page 106) will provide the perfect contrast to the spicy flavours here.

Hints and variations This recipe can be made in advance and reheated in the oven or microwave.

Leek and goats' cheese pie with tomato sauce

This warm and filling supper dish is particularly good served with Potato Stacks (page 109). For a lighter version, serve it with a fresh salad of sliced tomatoes dressed in vinaigrette instead of the sauce.

SERVES 8

225 g/8 oz shortcrust pastry (basic pie crust)

6 leeks, sliced

15 ml/1 tbsp sunflower oil

50 g/2 oz/¼ cup butter or margarine

100 g/4 oz/1 cup goats' cheese, crumbled

300 ml/½ pt/1¼ cups double (heavy) cream

2 eggs

Salt and freshly ground black pepper

225 g/8 oz puff pastry (paste)

1 small egg, beaten

FOR THE TOMATO SAUCE
30 ml/2 tbsp olive oil

1 small onion, finely chopped

1 small carrot, finely chopped

1 celery stick, finely chopped

200 g/7 oz/1 small can of chopped tomatoes

5 ml/1 tsp caster (superfine) sugar

1 Roll out the shortcrust pastry and use to line the base of a 23 cm/ 9 in pie dish.

2 Fry (sauté) the leeks gently in the oil and butter or margarine for 5 minutes, then spoon into the pie dish and top with the cheese.

3 Beat the cream and eggs together and pour this mixture into the pie dish. Season with salt and pepper.

4 Roll out the puff pastry to make a lid and top the pie with it. Glaze with beaten egg, then bake in a preheated oven at 200°C/400°F/ gas 6/fan oven 180°C for 40 minutes until the pie is golden.

5 While the pie is cooking, prepare the tomato sauce. Heat the oil and gently cook all the chopped vegetables for 5–6 minutes without browning.

6 Add the tomatoes and sugar, and season with salt and pepper. Return to the boil, then reduce the heat, cover and simmer for 20–25 minutes until thick. Boil, uncovered, for a few minutes if not thick enough.

7 Taste and adjust the seasoning before serving with the pie.

Preparation and cooking time 1 hour

Tabbouleh salad

This is a traditional Arab recipe, which can be varied by adding different salad ingredients and herbs, according to what you have available. Fresh herbs are crucial to the flavours.

SERVES 2

1 aubergine (eggplant), sliced

15 ml/1 tbsp olive oil

50 g/2 oz/½ cup bulghar (cracked wheat)

2 tomatoes, chopped

½ red onion, finely sliced

1 small garlic clove, crushed

2.5 ml/½ tsp salt

2.5 ml/½ tsp chopped fresh coriander (cilantro)

2.5 ml/½ tsp chopped fresh mint

Juice of ½ lemon

Salt and freshly ground black pepper

1 Drizzle the aubergine slices with olive oil and grill (broil) on both sides until brown. Allow to cool, then chop.

2 Pour boiling water little by little on to the bulghar until it is saturated (it should take about 60 ml/2 fl oz/¼ cup). Leave to stand until plumped up, then drain off any excess water.

3 Add the aubergine and all the other ingredients, mixing together.

4 Taste and adjust the seasoning.

Preparation and cooking time 15 minutes

Serving suggestions Tabbouleh is so versatile – you can serve it as a main vegetarian dish in its own right, perhaps with a tomato salad, but it also makes a perfect side dish.

Fresh tagliatelle with a spinach and mushroom sauce

This little recipe is easy and quick. Just make sure you use good-quality, fresh vegetables and you'll have a classy meal made in minutes. You can use other types of pasta if you wish.

SERVES 2

100 g/4 oz mushrooms, cleaned and sliced

30 ml/2 tbsp olive oil

100 g/4 oz cherry tomatoes, halved

150 g/5 oz fresh spinach leaves, washed and chopped

1 small garlic clove, finely chopped

10 ml/2 tsp pesto

45 ml/3 tbsp crème fraîche

A pinch of freshly grated nutmeg

250 g/9 oz fresh tagliatelle

15 g/¹/₂ oz/1 tbsp butter or margarine

Freshly ground black pepper

TO GARNISH
Shavings of Parmesan cheese

1 Fry (sauté) the mushrooms in the olive oil for 3–5 minutes until golden, then add the cherry tomatoes, spinach and garlic and cook until softened. Continue frying and add the pesto, crème fraîche and nutmeg. Turn the heat down to the lowest setting to keep warm.

2 Cook the tagliatelle in boiling, lightly salted water, then drain and toss in the butter or margarine and add a good grinding of black pepper.

3 Divide between two plates and top with the sauce. Garnish with a few shavings of Parmesan.

Preparation and cooking time 20 minutes

Serving suggestions This goes well with a green or mixed salad, or you could offer a plain green vegetable, if you prefer.

Potato and tomato gratin with pesto and crème fraîche

The mixture of fresh tomatoes and creamy potatoes makes this gratin lovely to look at. It's always popular and, best of all, it's very easy to prepare.

SERVES 4–6

1 kg/2¼ lb potatoes, thinly sliced

700 g/1½ lb vine tomatoes, peeled if preferred

60 ml/4 tbsp pesto

Salt and freshly ground black pepper

120 ml/4 fl oz/½ cup crème fraîche

1 Cook the potatoes in boiling, salted water for 10 minutes, then drain. Slice the tomatoes.

2 Arrange the slices of potato and tomato in alternate layers in a gratin dish, spreading the pesto between the layers. Season with salt and pepper and pour over the crème fraîche.

3 Cook the gratin in a preheated oven at 200°C/400°F/gas 6/fan oven 180°C for about 40 minutes until the potatoes are tender.

Preparation and cooking time 55 minutes

Serving suggestions I wouldn't offer anything more complicated than a green salad with this dish.

Baked courgettes with cheese and sweetcorn

Despite the simple ingredients, it's surprising how rich and filling this dish is. It's also very colourful and healthy, so it should be popular with all your guests.

SERVES 4

175 g/6 oz/1½ cups sweetcorn (corn)

100 g/4 oz/½ cup cottage cheese

Salt and freshly ground black pepper

2 shallots, finely chopped

4 courgettes (zucchini), halved lengthways and seeds removed

45 ml/3 tbsp freshly grated Parmesan cheese

1 Mix together the sweetcorn, cheese, salt, pepper and shallots.

2 Spoon the mixture into the courgette halves, mounding it up a little. Top with the Parmesan cheese.

3 Put the courgettes into a greased shallow ovenproof dish and bake in a preheated oven at 200°C/400°F/gas 6/fan oven 180°C for 15 minutes until tender and the topping has melted.

Preparation and cooking time 25 minutes

Serving suggestions Good accompaniments for this are sautéed potatoes and French Beans with Onion and Garlic (page 95) or a green salad.

Hints and variations This is also good made with Boursin instead of cottage cheese.

Garlic-roast vegetables with rosemary

This brightly coloured mix of vegetables tastes as good as it looks. It makes a great meal on its own and can also be served as a side dish for eight people. It is especially good with grilled meats.

SERVES 4

60 ml/4 tbsp olive oil

2 garlic cloves

2 red chillies, seeded and cut in half

4 sprigs of fresh rosemary

900 g/2 lb baby new potatoes, thinly sliced

900 g/2 lb cauliflower, cut into bite-sized pieces

2 red (bell) peppers, cut into chunky pieces

450 g/1 lb fresh spinach leaves, washed and patted dry

Salt and freshly ground black pepper

1 Put the oil in a shallow frying pan (skillet) together with the chilli, one of the garlic cloves and one of the sprigs of rosemary. Warm gently to flavour the oil.

2 Meanwhile, cook the potatoes and cauliflower in boiling, lightly salted water for 5 minutes.

3 When the oil is hot, discard the flavourings and add the chopped pepper, frying (sautéing) gently for a couple of minutes.

4 Drain the cooked cauliflower and potatoes and tip into the frying pan, then cook on a medium heat, stirring from time to time, for about 8 minutes.

5 Meanwhile, strip the leaves from the second sprig of rosemary and chop the remaining garlic clove. When the vegetables are cooked to your taste, add the rosemary and garlic to the pan with the spinach and cook for another minute or so.

6 Season with salt and pepper just before serving.

Preparation and cooking time 20 minutes

Serving suggestions All this needs is some warm granary rolls. You could serve a fresh tomato sauce (page 85) as an optional extra.

Spinach and ricotta parcels

These lovely little parcels look light as a feather but they make a quite substantial meal. The spinach and ricotta are a traditional Mediterranean combination – very tasty and full of goodness, too.

SERVES 4

350 g/12 oz fresh spinach leaves, washed and roughly chopped

1 small onion, finely chopped

25 g/1 oz/2 tbsp butter or margarine

5 ml/1 tsp whole green peppercorns

Salt

500 g/18 oz puff pastry (paste)

250 g/9 oz/generous 1 cup ricotta cheese

1 egg, beaten

TO GARNISH
Sprigs of fresh herbs

1 Put the washed spinach in a dry pan with just the water clinging to it and cook until wilted. Drain, cool and squeeze out any excess moisture.

2 Fry (sauté) the onion gently in the butter or margarine until softened but not browned. Add the green peppercorns and cook for 2–3 minutes. Remove from the heat and add the spinach, mixing together. Season lightly with salt.

3 Roll out the pastry thinly and cut into four squares about 15 cm/6 in across. Place a quarter of the spinach mixture in the centre of each square and top with a quarter of the cheese. Brush a little of the beaten egg around the edges of the pastry and bring the corners together to seal.

4 Brush the parcels with beaten egg and cook in a preheated oven at 200°C/400°F/gas 6/fan oven 180°C for 20–25 minutes.

5 Serve garnished with sprigs of fresh herbs.

Preparation and cooking time 30–35 minutes

Serving suggestions Arrange each parcel on a bed of Warm Bean Salad (page 94), accompanied by one or two Potato Stacks (page 109).

Vegetarian goulash

This vegetarian version is just as substantial as its meat counterpart. The caraway seeds and Marmite add a lovely flavour and aroma. You can vary the combination of vegetables depending on what is available. See photograph opposite page 97.

SERVES 4

1 onion, finely chopped

30 ml/2 tbsp sunflower oil

1 courgette (zucchini), diced

3 carrots, diced

2 parsnips, diced

2 celery sticks, sliced

5 ml/1 tsp paprika

2.5 ml/'½ tsp dried basil

2.5 ml/'½ tsp caraway seeds

30 ml/2 tbsp chopped fresh parsley

5 ml/1 tsp Marmite (yeast extract)

600 ml/1 pt/2½ cups passata (sieved tomatoes)

450 ml/¾ pt/2 cups vegetable stock

12 small potatoes

Salt and freshly ground black pepper

150 ml/'¼ pt/²⁄₃ cup plain yoghurt

1 Fry (sauté) the onion in the oil until softened but not browned. Add the courgette, carrots, parsnips and celery. Cover and cook for 10 minutes over a gentle heat.

2 Stir in all the remaining ingredients except the seasoning and yoghurt. Bring to the boil, then reduce the heat and simmer for 20–30 minutes.

3 Season to taste with salt and pepper, then stir in the yoghurt.

4 Garnish with parsley and serve.

Preparation and cooking time 40–50 minutes

Serving suggestions Serve either on a bed of plain ribbon noodles, or with some warm bread. Fried Peas with Garlic (page 101) make a good accompaniment.

Mushroom pilaff with cashew nuts

When I was trying out all my recipes before starting work in France, my brother Tim gave me this recipe. It has remained one of my favourites ever since I first tasted it, with its subtle oriental flavour.

SERVES 4

100 g/4 oz/½ cup brown rice

1 onion, sliced

A little sunflower oil

1 garlic clove, crushed

2 celery sticks, sliced

225 g/8 oz mushrooms, sliced

1 red (bell) pepper, sliced

1 green pepper, sliced

100 g/4 oz/1 cup raw cashew nuts

A dash of soy sauce

1 Cook the rice according to the packet directions.

2 Fry (sauté) the onion gently in the oil for 5 minutes until softened.

3 Add the garlic, celery, mushrooms, peppers and nuts. Mix together and fry for 2 minutes.

4 Add the soy sauce to taste, remembering that it is very salty, and cook for 5 minutes.

5 Add the cooked rice, stir well and heat through before serving.

Preparation and cooking time 40 minutes

Serving suggestions I like to serve this with a salad made of beansprouts tossed with some sliced or diced tomatoes.

sides dishes, garnishes and sauces

Many dishes are complemented perfectly well with plain boiled or steamed vegetables as side dishes and this is obviously the easiest option. But if you really want to impress your guests, this section is full of exciting combinations for you to try. They look and taste delicious and, what's more, most of them can be prepared in advance and then either cooked with the main course in the oven or simply reheated at the last minute in a pan or in the microwave. To keep things relatively simple when serving a more complicated accompaniment, opt for a straightforward main dish, such as plain grilled chops or steaks. I have also included some clever ideas for garnishing vegetables and a few favourite sauces.

Warm bean salad

This salad is served just warm. If you have any left and want to serve it at another meal, remember to bring it to room temperature before serving so that the full flavour can be appreciated.

SERVES 4

30 ml/2 tbsp wine vinegar

90 ml/6 tbsp olive oil

10 ml/2 tsp wholegrain mustard

Salt and freshly ground black pepper

2 shallots, finely sliced

450 g/1 lb young yellow or green beans, cut into short lengths

1 Mix together the vinegar, oil, mustard, salt and pepper to make a vinaigrette.

2 Place the shallots in the vinaigrette and marinate for 30 minutes. This makes them mild.

3 Boil the beans in salted water until just tender – not crisp and not mushy.

4 Drain and refresh briefly in cold water, then toss them in the vinaigrette while they are still warm.

Preparation and cooking time 10 minutes plus marinating

Refried beans

This recipe is a variation of the refried beans eaten with chilli beef and tortillas. It is deceptively simple and absolutely delicious.

SERVES 3–4

425 g/15 oz/1 large can of haricot (navy) beans

60 ml/4 tbsp olive oil

2 garlic cloves, crushed

Salt and freshly ground black pepper

TO GARNISH

Chopped fresh coriander (cilantro) or parsley

1 Tip the beans into a sieve (strainer). Drain, then rinse and drain again.

2 Put all the ingredients into a shallow frying pan (skillet) and cook over a low heat, stirring to blend them all together. When heated through, continue cooking for a further 5–6 minutes so that the beans become slightly mushy.

3 Serve garnished with chopped coriander or parsley.

Preparation and cooking time 15 minutes

French beans with onions and garlic

Beans are at their best when really fresh, so buy and cook them on the same day if you can. It that's not practical, you can keep them for a day in the salad crisper at the bottom of the fridge.

SERVES 4

450 g/1 lb French (green) beans

1 small onion, finely chopped

25 g/1 oz/2 tbsp butter or margarine

1 garlic clove, crushed

Salt and freshly ground black pepper

1 Cook the beans in boiling, lightly salted water until just tender.

2 Fry (sauté) the onion in the butter or margarine until softened but not browned. Add the garlic and cook very gently for 30 seconds. Do not allow to brown.

3 Drain the beans, toss with the onion and garlic, season to taste and serve.

Preparation and cooking time 10 minutes

French beans with bacon and spring onions

This is an unusual, but very simple, way to add interest to French beans. It is equally delicious with frozen peas, which is handy for last-minute accompaniments!

SERVES 4

450 g/1 lb French (green) beans

2 rashers (slices) of streaky bacon, cut into pieces

50 g/2 oz/¼ cup butter or margarine

6 spring onions (scallions), chopped

8 lettuce leaves, shredded

A pinch of caster (superfine) sugar

Salt and freshly ground black pepper

TO GARNISH
Chopped fresh mint or parsley

1 Parboil the beans for 3 minutes, then drain.

2 Cook the bacon in the butter or margarine. Add the beans, spring onions, lettuce and sugar, and season with salt and pepper. Cover and continue cooking, stirring occasionally, until the beans are tender.

3 Serve garnished with mint or parsley.

Preparation and cooking time 15 minutes

French beans with feta and sun-dried tomatoes

For a really full, rich flavour, use sun-dried tomatoes packed in olive oil for this recipe. Although you drain off the oil before slicing the tomatoes, they have absorbed the wonderful flavours.

SERVES 6

350 g/12 oz frozen French (green) beans

50 g/2 oz/½ cup sun-dried tomatoes, sliced

15 ml/1 tbsp oil from the jar of tomatoes

100 g/4 oz/1 cup feta cheese, crumbled

Salt and freshly ground black pepper

1 Cook the beans according to the packet directions, then drain well.

2 Toss together with the remaining ingredients over a gentle heat. Serve immediately.

Preparation and cooking time 10 minutes

Soy garlic beans

The oriental flavour of these beans goes surprisingly well with Mediterranean meat and fish dishes so do give the dish a try. It is simplicity itself to prepare.

SERVES 4

450 g/1 lb frozen French (green) beans

15 ml/1 tbsp sunflower oil

15 g/½ oz/1 tbsp butter or margarine, softened

2 garlic cloves, chopped

15 ml/1 tbsp soy sauce

A pinch of caster (superfine) sugar

250 ml/8 fl oz/1 cup water

1 Fry (sauté) the beans in the oil and butter or margarine for 3 minutes.

2 Sprinkle the garlic, soy sauce and sugar over the beans and pour over the water. Bring to the boil and boil rapidly until the liquid has evaporated.

3 Serve at once.

Preparation and cooking time 10 minutes

Photograph opposite:
Fruits de Mer en Papillote (see page 72)

Steamed broccoli with garlic and mustard seeds

The simplest ways of cooking vegetables are often the best, as you want them to retain their nutrients and their fresh colours and flavours. Broccoli, in particular, can be served quite crisp.

SERVES 6

900 g/2 lb broccoli, cut into even-sized florets

10 ml/2 tsp yellow mustard seeds

75 ml/5 tbsp olive oil

2–3 garlic cloves, crushed

2.5 ml/¹/₂ tsp salt

1 Steam the broccoli until just tender, then rinse immediately in cold water.

2 Just before serving, fry (sauté) the mustard seeds in the oil. When they pop, stir in the garlic.

3 Add the broccoli and salt. Stir gently to mix and cook until heated through and glistening.

Preparation and cooking time 10 minutes

Cabbage with nutmeg

Cabbage often gets a bad press, but I think it's the fault of the cook, not the ingredient! The secret is not to overcook it. See photograph opposite page 48.

SERVES 8

1 Savoy cabbage, shredded and washed

45 ml/3 tbsp double (heavy) cream

A good pinch of freshly grated nutmeg

Salt and freshly ground black pepper

1 Cook the cabbage in boiling, lightly salted water for 2 minutes.

2 Drain and return to the pan and stir in the cream, nutmeg, salt and pepper to taste.

3 Reheat gently, then serve at once.

Preparation and cooking time 10 minutes

SIDE DISHES, GARNISHES AND SAUCES

Photograph opposite:
Vegetarian Goulash (see page 91)
with ribbon noodles

Turkish fried carrots

These carrots are perfect with roast lamb or any plain grilled fish or meat. Because they are such a sweet vegetable, they fry beautifully, and are always a good colour choice for a stunning presentation.

SERVES 4

450 g/1 lb carrots, sliced

15 ml/1 tbsp seasoned flour

30 ml/2 tbsp olive oil

Salt and freshly ground black pepper

300 ml/½ pt/1¼ cups plain yoghurt

A good pinch of garam masala

TO GARNISH
Chopped fresh mint

1 Cook the carrots in boiling, lightly salted water, then drain and cool. When cold, spread on kitchen paper (paper towels) to dry.

2 Toss the carrots in the seasoned flour and shake off any surplus.

3 Fry (sauté) in the oil until golden brown. Season to taste with salt and pepper and keep warm on a serving dish.

4 Put the yoghurt into a small pan and heat very gently. Pour over the carrots, sprinkle on the garam masala and garnish with mint.

Preparation and cooking time 20 minutes

Baby carrots with orange and cardamom

You need to cook carrots so that they are tender but still have some bite. The days of boiling the life out of our vegetables are long gone – thank goodness!

SERVES 4–6

700 g/1½ lb baby carrots, topped and tailed

150 ml/¼ pt/⅔ cup thick plain yoghurt

Juice of 1 large orange

3 green cardamoms, crushed

30 ml/2 tbsp olive oil

Salt and freshly ground black pepper

1 Boil or steam the carrots for 10–12 minutes until just tender. Drain and turn them into a deep dish.

2 Mix the yoghurt, orange juice, cardamoms and olive oil with a pinch of salt and pepper and quickly stir the mixture into the carrots. Serve hot, warm or cold.

Preparation and cooking time 20 minutes

Garlic carrots and courgettes with lime

This is a really quick dish to cook as the vegetables are grated. If you are entertaining – or even if you are not! – have everything prepared in advance, then you can cook it quickly and simply.

SERVES 4

15 ml/1 tbsp oil

25 g/1 oz/2 tbsp butter or margarine

2 courgettes (zucchini), grated

2 carrots, grated

2 garlic cloves, crushed

Grated zest of 1 lime

Salt and freshly ground black pepper

Juice of ½ lime

5 ml/1 tsp dried thyme

1 In a large frying pan (skillet), heat the oil and butter or margarine. Add the grated vegetables and garlic and fry (sauté), stirring, for 2 minutes.

2 Add the lime zest and season to taste with salt and pepper. Stir in the lime juice and thyme and continue to cook for a further 5–6 minutes until all the flavours have combined. Serve hot.

Preparation and cooking time 20 minutes

Steamed cauliflower with almonds

Don't overcook the cauliflower. It should be tender but still with just a little bite. The buttered almonds then give a lovely, complementary texture and flavour.

SERVES 4

1 large cauliflower, cut into florets

Salt

50 g/2 oz/½ cup flaked (slivered) almonds

50 g/2 oz/¼ cup unsalted (sweet) butter

1 Steam the cauliflower until almost tender but not soft. Drain, if necessary, and season very lightly with salt.

2 Fry (sauté) the almonds in the butter until golden brown. Spoon over the cooked cauliflower and serve.

Preparation and cooking time 15 minutes

Creamy courgette bake

This is my all-time favourite courgette recipe and makes a wonderful creamy accompaniment to any plain meat or fish. You could use a mixture of yellow and green courgettes for added variety.

SERVES 4

450 g/1 lb courgettes (zucchini), grated

5 ml/1 tsp salt

5 ml/1 tsp caster (superfine) sugar

10 ml/2 tbsp tarragon vinegar

A little butter or margarine, for greasing

1 egg

300 ml/½ pt/1¼ cups double (heavy) cream

6 basil leaves, torn

15 ml/1 tbsp freshly grated Parmesan cheese

1 Toss the courgettes in a large bowl with the salt, sugar and vinegar. Cover and leave in a cool place for several hours.

2 Drain the courgettes very well, squeezing them to get rid of all the juice – this is very important.

3 Put them in a lightly greased gratin dish and fluff them up with a fork.

4 Beat the egg lightly with the cream, the torn basil leaves and the grated Parmesan and pour over the courgettes.

5 Bake in a preheated oven at 200°C/400°F/gas 6/fan oven 180°C for about 20 minutes until the custard is set around the edges but still slightly creamy in the centre.

Preparation and cooking time 25 minutes plus standing

Courgette patties

These also make a delicious starter, served with either a fresh tomato sauce (see page 85) or mayonnaise flavoured with garlic and herbs. You can make them larger as a side dish, or bite-sized for a starter.

SERVES 4

4–6 courgettes (zucchini), grated

40 g/1½ oz/⅓ cup plain (all-purpose) flour

2 eggs, lightly beaten

2.5 ml/½ tsp salt

A pinch of freshly ground black pepper

25 g/1 oz/2 tbsp butter or margarine

30 ml/2 tbsp sunflower oil

1 Mix the courgettes with the flour, eggs, salt and a pinch of pepper to form a batter.

2 Heat the butter or margarine with the oil in a frying pan (skillet) and add spoonfuls of the batter to form patties about 5 cm/2 in in diameter, flattening each one slightly with the back of a spoon.

3 Cook in batches for about 4 minutes on each side until golden brown and crisp.

4 Drain on kitchen paper (paper towels) and keep warm.

5 Serve hot.

Preparation and cooking time 5 minutes plus 8 minutes' cooking per batch

Hints and variations If you need to add more oil when cooking the patties, make sure you heat it fully before adding the next batch.

Fried peas with garlic

This simple recipe is a brilliant way of transforming a packet of frozen peas into a really special-tasting accompaniment. The quantities don't matter.

SERVES 4

225 g/8 oz/2 cups frozen peas

Butter or margarine, for cooking

A little caster (superfine) sugar

Salt and freshly ground black pepper

Crushed garlic, to taste

1 Fry (sauté) frozen peas in plenty of butter or margarine.

2 After 2 minutes, add a little sugar, lots of black pepper and crushed garlic to taste.

3 Cover and cook gently for about 5 minutes until the peas are tender.

Preparation and cooking time About 10 minutes

Braised fennel with garlic and cream

This is a great accompaniment to any fish course. Use a chicken, meat or vegetable stock if you want to serve it with other dishes – it's delicious with poultry and meat dishes too. See photograph opposite page 120.

SERVES 4

4 fennel bulbs

45 ml/3 tbsp olive oil

1 onion, finely sliced

4 garlic cloves, chopped

Salt and freshly ground black pepper

5 ml/1 tsp fish stock powder

20 ml/4 tsp single (light) cream

1 Remove the tough outer layer from the fennel and cut the bulbs into slices. Reserve the leafy green fronds for garnish.

2 Warm the olive oil in a saucepan and gently cook the sliced onion until softened, without allowing it to colour. Add the garlic and sliced fennel, then season to taste with salt and pepper.

3 Add the stock powder with 10 ml/2 tsp of water, cover and cook gently for 20 minutes, then add the cream and continue cooking for a further 10 minutes.

4 Serve garnished with the reserved fennel fronds.

Preparation and cooking time 40 minutes

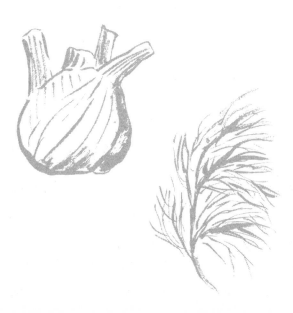

Baked fennel with fresh tomatoes

This casserole of vegetables with its juicy sauce is an ideal accompaniment to grilled meat or fish. It takes only minutes to prepare, then you can leave it in the oven to do its own thing until you are ready to serve.

SERVES 4

6 garlic cloves, crushed

30 ml/2 tbsp olive oil, plus extra for cooking

4 fennel bulbs, thickly sliced

25 g/1 oz/¼ cup plain (all-purpose) flour

450 g/1 lb juicy tomatoes, cut into quarters

10 ml/2 tsp caster (superfine) sugar

Salt and freshly ground black pepper

10 ml/2 tsp dried thyme

1 In a frying pan (skillet), fry (sauté) the garlic in the oil until browned. Transfer to a casserole dish (Dutch oven).

2 Dip the fennel in the flour to coat, then fry in the frying pan until golden. Transfer to the casserole.

3 Heat a little more oil in the frying pan, then add the tomatoes and sugar. Season with salt and pepper and bring to the boil. Turn into the casserole dish and sprinkle with the thyme.

4 Cover and cook in a preheated oven at 180°C/350°F/gas 4/fan oven 160°C for 1 hour.

Preparation and cooking time About 1¼ hours

Braised leeks in vermouth

These leeks are a fine accompaniment to any chicken dish. Although of the onion family, they have a much more subtle flavour, which works well when simmered with the vermouth and stock.

SERVES 2

15 g/½ oz/1 tbsp butter or margarine

1 small leek, thinly sliced

100 ml/3½ fl oz/scant ½ cup dry white vermouth

100 ml/3½ fl oz/scant ½ cup chicken stock

Salt and freshly ground black pepper

1 Melt the butter or margarine in a saucepan and add the leek, cooking gently until softened.

2 Pour in the vermouth, then boil rapidly to boil off the alcohol.

3 Add the chicken stock, reduce the heat and simmer for 5 minutes until tender. Season to taste before serving.

Preparation and cooking time 15 minutes

Piquant leeks with orange

This is a lovely way to dress leeks up and makes a delicious accompaniment for pork, chicken and fish. The dash of lemon juice just finishes off the flavours.

SERVES 6

5 large leeks, trimmed and washed

40 g/1½ oz/3 tbsp butter or margarine

Grated zest and juice of 1 orange

Salt and freshly ground black pepper

40 g/1½ oz/⅓ cup plain (all-purpose) flour

300 ml/½ pt/1¼ cups milk, plus a little extra

A dash of lemon juice

1 Cut the leeks into 5 cm/2 in lengths and finely shred them.

2 Melt the butter or margarine in a frying pan (skillet) and add the leeks and orange juice and season with salt and pepper.

3 Cover and simmer for about 10 minutes.

4 Remove the lid and boil off most of the liquid.

5 Sprinkle the flour over the buttery juices and stir to combine thoroughly.

6 Gradually add the milk and orange zest, stirring all the time.

7 Heat the mixture gently and simmer for 4–5 minutes until thick and creamy, if necessary thinning with the extra milk. Season again and add the lemon juice before serving.

Preparation and cooking time 25 minutes

Lemon potatoes

I find this potato dish particularly suitable when cooking for larger numbers of people but the quantities are easily reduced when you are cooking for just you and the family.

SERVES 8

1.75 kg/4 lb potatoes, diced

100 g/4 oz/½ cup butter or margarine

2 onions, finely chopped

Grated zest and juice of 2 lemons

60 ml/4 tbsp chopped fresh parsley

Salt and freshly ground black pepper

1 Cover the potatoes with cold water, bring to the boil, then reduce the heat and simmer for 3 minutes. Tip into a sieve (strainer) and drain well.

2 Melt the butter or margarine in the empty pan. Add the onions and fry (sauté) until softened but not browned. Stir in the lemon zest and juice, the parsley, salt and pepper.

3 Return the potatoes to the pan and toss gently to coat in the mixture. Put into a shallow ovenproof dish (they can be left like this all day in a cool place if needed).

4 Bake in a preheated oven at 190°C/375°F/gas 5/fan oven 170°C for about 1 hour until they are golden brown and crisp on top.

Preparation and cooking time 1¼ hours

Sugar-browned potatoes

These glazed potatoes are irresistible with any grilled meat or fish. Keep an eye on the pan while you are cooking, so that the butter and sugar don't overbrown.

SERVES 4–6

900 g/2 lb small potatoes

25 g/1 oz/1 tbsp caster (superfine) sugar

50 g/2 oz/¼ cup unsalted (sweet) butter

1 Cook the potatoes in boiling, lightly salted water until tender, then drain.

2 Heat the sugar and butter in a frying pan (skillet) until caramelised.

3 Rinse the potatoes in cold water and drain well once more before adding to the frying pan. Continue cooking over a low heat, shaking the pan gently, until the potatoes are evenly glazed and golden brown.

4 Serve hot.

Preparation and cooking time 25 minutes

Classic potatoes with cream

These are delicious served with any plain meat or fish dish that requires a moist vegetable. They are versatile and very user-friendly as you can cook them and reheat later if you wish.

SERVES 4

4 potatoes

Salt and freshly ground black pepper

Butter or margarine, for greasing and topping

1 garlic clove, crushed

A little freshly grated nutmeg

300 ml/½ pt/1¼ cups single (light) cream

1 Slice the potatoes thinly and sprinkle with salt. Leave to stand for 5–10 minutes and then squeeze out excess water.

2 Grease a shallow ovenproof dish and rub it with a crushed garlic clove. Layer the potatoes in the dish, sprinkle with nutmeg and pepper between each layer, and pour enough cream to reach the top layer. Top with dots of butter or margarine.

3 Bake uncovered in a preheated oven at 140°C/275°F/gas 1/fan oven 125°C for at least 1 hour, preferably longer.

4 Cook under a hot grill (broiler) until golden brown on top before serving.

Preparation and cooking time At least 1¼ hours

Hints and variations However much you are making, always use a shallow dish. Do not be tempted to make the layers too deep, or they will take too long to cook through, and always allow plenty of time for cooking. Put them in as early as possible and if they are ready too soon, just remove from the oven and reheat later.

SIDE DISHES, GARNISHES AND SAUCES

Swedish potatoes

Being a Scandinavian dish, these potatoes are traditionally served with a plate of smoked salmon, but they are delicious served as an accompaniment to any fish – especially smoked varieties.

SERVES 4

700 g/1½ lb new potatoes, scraped

15 ml/1 tbsp olive oil

25 g/1 oz/2 tbsp butter or margarine

40 g/1½ oz/⅓ cup plain (all-purpose) flour

300 ml/½ pt/1¼ cups milk

5 ml/1 tsp dried dill (dill weed)

5 ml/1 tsp dill seed

15 ml/1 tbsp chopped fresh parsley

30 ml/2 tbsp lemon juice

Salt and freshly ground black pepper

1 Place the potatoes in a pan of boiling, lightly salted water. Add the oil. Bring back to the boil and cook for about 20 minutes until the potatoes are tender. Drain and keep warm.

2 Melt the butter or margarine in a saucepan and blend in the flour. Gradually add the milk, stirring constantly. Add the dried dill and dill seed and cook, stirring, until the sauce starts to thicken. Add the parsley and lemon juice, and season with salt and pepper.

3 Beat the sauce well and add the potatoes. Heat through for 2 minutes, then turn into a warmed dish and serve.

Preparation and cooking time 30 minutes

Potato patties

A great way to use up leftover cooked potatoes, these are easy to prepare, and can be made in advance and frozen. Because they are baked, rather than fried, they absorb less fat, so everyone can afford to have 'just one more'.

SERVES 4

500 g/18 oz potatoes, cooked and mashed

30 ml/2 tbsp chopped fresh parsley

5 ml/1 tsp chopped fresh sage

30 ml/2 tbsp olive oil, plus extra for brushing

Salt and freshly ground black pepper

1 Preheat the oven to 220°C/425°F/gas 7/fan oven 200°C and lightly grease a baking (cookie) sheet.

2 Mix the potatoes with the herbs and oil, then season with salt and pepper.

3 Shape into four rounds, flatten the tops and place on the baking sheet. Brush with a little more oil and bake for 15 minutes until crisp and golden.

Preparation and cooking time 20 minutes

Antibes potatoes

Because you boil the potatoes before you roast them, they end up soft in the centre and crisp on the outside, and absorb much less fat than conventional chips.

SERVES 3–4

450 g/1 lb potatoes, scrubbed

A little sunflower oil

Salt and freshly ground black pepper

15 ml/1 tbsp chopped fresh mixed herbs

1 Cut the potatoes into thick fingers and boil them for about 5 minutes until they are nearly tender. Drain and put into a roasting tin (pan).

2 Drizzle over just enough oil to coat the chips (fries). Season with salt and pepper and sprinkle over the chopped herbs. Toss lightly.

3 Bake in a preheated oven at 230°C/450°F/gas 8/fan oven 210°C for about 20 minutes until golden brown.

Preparation and cooking time 30 minutes

Garlic rosti

Because these potatoes are baked, rather than fried, they are nice and crisp without being greasy. Make sure you cut the potatoes into even-sized pieces so they all cook in the same time. See photograph opposite page 48.

SERVES 4

700 g/1½ lb potatoes

50 g/2 oz/¼ cup butter or margarine

1 medium onion, finely chopped

3 large garlic cloves, finely chopped

Salt and freshly ground black pepper

1 Cut the potatoes into equal-sized pieces and boil in lightly salted water for 10 minutes. Drain and cool.

2 In a large pan, melt the butter or margarine, add the onion and cook gently for 4–5 minutes until softened but not browned. Add the garlic and continue cooking for another minute or so.

3 Coarsely grate the cooled potatoes and add them to the onion and garlic mixture. Season to taste with salt and pepper.

4 Divide the mixture into 12 portions and put into patty tins (pans) or a flat ovenproof dish.

5 Bake in a preheated oven at 190°C/375°F/gas 5/fan oven 170°C for 35–40 minutes until crisp and golden.

Preparation and cooking time 1 hour

Potato stacks

These crisp, golden potato stacks are always a hit – they taste as good as they look.

SERVES 4

65 g/2½ oz/scant ⅓ cup butter or margarine

1 garlic clove, crushed

Salt and freshly ground black pepper

450 g/1 lb potatoes

1 Melt the butter or margarine in a frying pan (skillet). Stir in the crushed garlic and season well with salt and pepper.

2 Peel and thinly slice the potatoes. Do not rinse them – the starch will help the stacks stick together. Stir in the garlic butter.

3 Stack the potato slices on a baking (cookie) sheet, to form four 10 cm/4 in rounds.

4 Cook in a preheated oven at 200°C/400°F/gas 6/fan oven 180°C for 30–40 minutes or until golden brown and tender.

Preparation and cooking time 35–45 minutes

Festive sweet and sour onions with passata

These tender little onions go well with poultry of any kind and would make an interesting addition to your usual Christmas dinner. The tomatoes give the onions a lovely rich colour and flavour.

SERVES 6

1 kg/2¼ lb button (pearl) onions

400 ml/14 fl oz/1¾ cups passata (sieved tomatoes)

100 g/4 oz/½ cup soft brown sugar

30 ml/2 tbsp olive oil

60 ml/4 tbsp red wine vinegar

2.5 ml/½ tsp dried thyme

Freshly ground black pepper

1 Peel the onions, then blanch for 10 minutes in boiling, lightly salted water. Drain and tip into a shallow ovenproof dish.

2 Mix all the other ingredients together and pour over the onions.

3 Bake in the oven at 180°C/350°F/gas 4/fan oven 160°C for 1 hour, basting occasionally.

Preparation and cooking time 1 hour 20 minutes

Glazed shallots

These sweet glazed shallots are an ideal accompaniment to roast lamb or other roast or grilled meats.

SERVES 4

12 shallots, unpeeled

15 ml/1 tbsp olive oil

15 g/½ oz/1 tbsp butter or margarine

5 ml/1 tsp caster (superfine) sugar

Salt and freshly ground black pepper

TO GARNISH
Chopped fresh parsley

1 Put the shallots into a pan of boiling water, cover, reduce the heat and simmer for 3 minutes. Drain and rinse in cold water, then remove the skins, leaving the root intact. This ensures the insides of the shallots do not pop out during cooking.

2 Heat the oil and butter or margarine in a heavy-based pan. Add the sugar and shallots and cook for 15–20 minutes, shaking the pan occasionally, until the shallots are brown.

3 Season with salt and pepper and sprinkle with the parsley.

Preparation and cooking time 20–25 minutes

Creamed spinach

Cook spinach for just long enough to allow it to wilt and absorb the flavours of the other ingredients. That way it will keep its vibrant colour and all its nutritional value. Be prepared for it to reduce considerably in volume.

SERVES 6

50 g/2 oz/¼ cup unsalted (sweet) butter

1 kg/2¼ lb frozen leaf spinach, thawed and drained

2 garlic cloves, crushed

A good pinch of freshly grated nutmeg

Salt and freshly ground black pepper

120 ml/4 fl oz/½ cup double (heavy) cream

1 Melt the butter in a pan and add the drained spinach, garlic, plenty of nutmeg, a little salt and a generous grinding of pepper.

2 Gradually add enough cream to give the spinach a creamy consistency. Gently heat through and serve.

Preparation and cooking time 5 minutes

Warm spinach salad

This is a great way to dress up spinach and has a lovely simple, fresh flavour. Just cook it until the leaves begin to wilt, don't steam it until it goes soggy.

SERVES 4

30 ml/2 tbsp olive oil

450 g/1 lb fresh spinach leaves, washed

Juice of ½ lemon

Salt and freshly ground black pepper

1 Heat the oil in a frying pan (skillet) and add the spinach. Stir over a gentle heat till wilted, then squeeze over the lemon juice and season to taste with salt and pepper.

2 Serve immediately.

Preparation and cooking time 5 minutes

Orange-glazed turnips

These orange-flavoured turnips go particularly well with rich meats like lamb, pork and duck. If you can't find baby turnips, you can make it just as successfully with chunks of full-sized turnip.

SERVES 4

700 g/1½ lb baby turnips, left whole

75 g/3 oz/⅓ cup butter or margarine

30 ml/2 tbsp caster (superfine) sugar

1 large red onion, cut into wedges

2 oranges, peeled and cut into segments

TO GARNISH
Snipped fresh chives

1 Cook the turnips in boiling, salted water for 10 minutes until tender, then drain.

2 Melt the butter or margarine and add the sugar, stirring over a gentle heat until dissolved.

3 Add the turnips and cook for 6–8 minutes over a high heat, stirring occasionally. Add the onion and orange segments and cook for a further 5 minutes.

4 Serve hot, garnished with snipped chives.

Preparation and cooking time 35 minutes

Kumquat and red onion marmalade

This delicious, sticky onion sauce combines the slightly tart flavour of kumquats with sweet red onions. It is delicious served with duck breasts and some fresh steamed green vegetables, as illustrated on the cover.

SERVES 4

25 g/1 oz/2 tbsp butter

3 red onions, thinly sliced

3 kumquats, thinly sliced

15 ml/1 tbsp demerara sugar

60 ml/4 tbsp caster (superfine) sugar

60 ml/4 tbsp orange juice

30 ml/2 tbsp red wine vinegar

1 Melt the butter in a saucepan, add the onions and fry (sauté), stirring, for 3 minutes. Add the kumquats and both the sugars and continue to cook, stirring occasionally, for about 5 minutes until the onions and kumquats are a deep golden brown.

2 Stir in the orange juice and the wine vinegar and stir for 1 minute until rich and thick.

3 Serve warm.

Preparation and cooking time 15 minutes

Glazed turnips with mustard

Turnips have the reputation of being rather dull, but cooking them like this gives them a lovely buttery taste, with the slight bite imparted by the mustard softened by the dash of sugar.

SERVES 6

900 g/2 lb whole baby turnips

50 g/2 oz/¹⁄₄ cup unsalted (sweet) butter

150 ml/¹⁄₄ pt/²⁄₃ cup chicken stock

5 ml/1 tsp soft brown sugar

Salt and freshly ground black pepper

10 ml/2 tsp French mustard

TO GARNISH
30 ml/2 tbsp chopped fresh parsley

1 Fry (sauté) the turnips in the butter, coating them well. Continue to cook over a moderate heat for about 10 minutes until they turn an even golden colour, like roast potatoes.

2 Add the stock and sugar and season to taste with salt and pepper. Bring to the boil, then reduce the heat, cover and simmer for 20 minutes, shaking occasionally, until tender.

3 Remove the turnips from the pan and stir the mustard into the pan juices, adding more sugar or seasoning to taste. Return the turnips to the pan, reheat and swirl around to coat in the buttery glaze.

4 Serve garnished with the parsley.

Preparation and cooking time 40 minutes

Italian vegetable bake

As you can see from the ingredients, this is a very robust dish and you could serve it as a meal in its own right. Just add a salad made with some fresh baby spinach leaves to complete the feast. See photograph opposite page 120.

SERVES 6

3 large potatoes, chopped

225 g/8 oz aubergines (eggplants), cut into bite-sized cubes

60 ml/4 tbsp olive oil

30 ml/2 tbsp chopped fresh parsley

100 g/4 oz/1 cup freshly grated Parmesan cheese

1 garlic clove, crushed

450 g/1 lb tomatoes, thinly sliced

75 g/3 oz/1½ cups fresh white breadcrumbs

Salt and freshly ground black pepper

1 Blanch the potatoes and aubergines in boiling, salted water for 3–4 minutes.

2 Drain and toss in 30 ml/2 tbsp of the oil and put into a deep ovenproof dish.

3 Mix together the parsley, cheese and garlic. Sprinkle this mixture over the vegetables and top with an overlapping layer of the sliced tomatoes.

4 Top with the breadcrumbs and drizzle the remaining olive oil over the top.

5 Season with salt and pepper and bake in a preheated oven at 220°C/425°F/gas 7/fan oven 200°C for 10 minutes.

6 Reduce the heat to 200°C/400°F/gas 6/fan oven 180°C and cook for a further 35 minutes until golden brown.

Preparation and cooking time 55 minutes

Anchovy cream

*This dressing is sufficient for 700 g/1½ lb new potatoes, or you can use it to dress
up plain grilled salmon. Even though there is a whole can of anchovies in the recipe,
the finished cream has only a very subtle hint of fish.*

SERVES 6

**50 g/2 oz/1 small can of
anchovy fillets in oil**

**150 ml/¼ pt/⅔ cup double
(heavy) cream**

Freshly ground black pepper

30 ml/2 tbsp snipped fresh chives

1 Chop the anchovies and put with their oil into a bowl over a pan of
simmering water. Heat and stir until they form a smooth paste.

2 Pour the cream into another pan and slowly bring to the boil, then
reduce the heat and simmer for 3–4 minutes. Remove from the heat,
add the anchovy paste, then leave to cool.

3 Season to taste with pepper, add the chives and use as required.

Preparation and cooking time 10 minutes

Anchovy vinaigrette

*This dressing is particularly good with hard-boiled eggs and juicy tomatoes, but it's
also excellent with French beans or a simple green salad.*

MAKES 150 ML/¼ PT/⅔ CUP

Salt and freshly ground black pepper

2.5 ml/½ tsp anchovy essence (extract)

5 ml/1 tsp French mustard

15 ml/1 tbsp wine vinegar

75 ml/5 tbsp olive oil

1 Whisk all the ingredients except the oil until blended.

2 Gradually add the oil, whisking all the time.

3 Use as required.

Preparation time 5 minutes

Honeyed leek sauce

*This sauce is a delicious accompaniment to any lamb dish. Stir any meat juices from
your accompanying main course into the sauce before pouring over the meat.*

MAKES 450 ML/³/₄ PT/2 CUPS

**350 g/12 oz leeks, trimmed and
finely chopped**

50 g/2 oz/¹/₄ cup unsalted (sweet) butter

15 ml/1 tbsp plain (all-purpose) flour

300 ml/¹/₂ pt/1¹/₄ cups chicken stock

75 ml/5 tbsp white wine

30 ml/2 tbsp white wine vinegar

30 ml/2 tbsp clear honey

30 ml/2 tbsp chopped fresh parsley

Salt and freshly ground black pepper

1 Fry (sauté) the leeks gently in the butter for about 5 minutes until
they are softened but not browned.

2 Add the flour and cook for another minute, then stir in the stock,
wine, vinegar and honey. Bring to the boil, reduce the heat and
simmer for 3 minutes.

3 Just before serving, add any pan juices, stir in the parsley and
season to taste with salt and pepper.

Preparation and cooking time 15 minutes

Tomato salsa

*This is a good relish to serve with plain grilled meat or fish, with burgers or a
barbecue. You could also serve it as a pre-dinner dip with corn chips or garlic bread.*

MAKES 450 ML/³/₄ PT/2 CUPS

**450 g/1 lb fresh tomatoes, seeded and
finely chopped**

10–15 ml/2–3 tsp caster (superfine) sugar

**¹/₂ small onion or 3–4 spring onions
(scallions), finely chopped**

2 garlic cloves, crushed

**1–2 green or red chillies, seeded and
finely chopped**

30 ml/2 tbsp olive oil

10 ml/2 tsp lemon or lime juice

Salt and freshly ground pepper

1 Combine all the ingredients except the salt and pepper in a small
bowl and leave at room temperature for 30 minutes for the flavours
to develop.

2 Season to taste with salt and pepper.

Preparation time 35 minutes

Top tips for dressing up vegetables

Try these tips to turn any plain cooked vegetable into a masterpiece.

- Apricot jam (conserve) stirred into cooked carrots gives a lovely fruity taste.

- Parsley and melted butter are excellent for carrots, potatoes and sweetcorn (corn) kernels.

- Toss carrots and leeks in orange cordial to give them an extra zip.

- Add a little chopped onion, fried (sautéed) until softened but not browned, to peas and beans.

- Browned fried onions are good with cauliflower.

- Fried or toasted nuts and/or raisins are excellent with sprouts, cauliflower, courgettes (zucchini), broccoli and rice.

- Chopped bacon, fried until crisp, makes a good addition to peas, beans, leeks and salads.

- Very thinly sliced red (bell) pepper adds bright colour to green vegetables.

- Tomatoes stewed with herbs complement French (green) beans and cauliflower beautifully.

- Fried mushrooms make an interesting addition to peas and sweetcorn (corn).

- Cream cheese and egg yolks make mashed potatoes taste rich and elegant.

- Cream, garlic and a hint of nutmeg give spinach a real lift.

- To add flavour to roast potatoes, toss in mustard powder before roasting as usual.

desserts

No dinner party would be complete without a dessert. As a rule, if I'm entertaining six or more guests, I offer a choice of sweets, making sure they are totally different in colour, texture and flavour. The trouble is that most people opt for a bit of both – so don't be too generous with the first portions!

Chocolate tart with rum

This tart has a light, crispy base and a delicious chocolate filling that is full of flavour without being too rich and heavy. I love the flavour of rum with chocolate, but you could use brandy if you prefer.

SERVES 6

225 g/8 oz sweet shortcrust pastry (basic pie crust)

3 whole eggs

1 egg yolk

100 g/4 oz/½ cup caster (superfine) sugar

225 g/8 oz plain (semi-sweet) chocolate

100 g/4 oz milk chocolate

50 g/2 oz/¼ cup unsalted (sweet) butter

25 ml/1 fl oz/1½ tbsp single (light) cream

50 ml/2 fl oz/3 tbsp dark rum

TO SERVE
Single (light) cream

1 Grease a 24 cm/9 in flan tin (pie pan), line with the pastry (paste) and set on a baking (cookie) sheet. Line the pastry with greaseproof (waxed) paper and top with baking beans. Bake blind in a preheated oven at 180°C/350°F/gas 5/fan oven 160°C for 20 minutes. Remove the beans and paper and leave to cool.

2 Whisk the eggs, egg yolk and sugar together until the mixture is pale and has doubled in volume.

3 Melt the chocolates, butter, cream and rum together in a bowl set over a pan of simmering water. Cool slightly, then fold into the egg mixture.

4 Pour into the cooked pastry case (pie shell) and bake for 15 minutes until the filling is set.

5 Allow to cool a little, then serve warm with a jug of single cream.

Preparation and cooking time 50 minutes

Hot raspberry brûlée

This effortless pudding tastes and looks mouth-wateringly delicious and can be made equally well with blueberries or sliced peaches. Mascarpone has a slightly sweet, rich flavour, which is perfect for this recipe.

SERVES 6

350 g/12 oz fresh or thawed frozen raspberries

300 g/11 oz/1⅓ cups Mascarpone cheese

100 g/4 oz/½ cup golden granulated sugar

1 Place the raspberries in a large, flat, flameproof dish.

2 Stir the Mascarpone cheese to soften it and then spread over the raspberries. If preparing in advance, chill until required.

3 When ready to cook, sprinkle the sugar over the top. Put under a grill (broiler), preheated to its hottest temperature, until the sugar has caramelised and you can see the fruit bubbling.

4 Serve immediately.

Preparation and cooking time 10 minutes

Hints and variations The Mascarpone cheese can be replaced by crème fraîche, or a mixture of double (heavy) cream and thick plain yoghurt.

If you use frozen raspberries, make sure they are top quality.

DESSERTS

Photograph opposite:
**Braised Fennel with Garlic and Cream (see page 102)
and Italian Vegetable Bake (see page 114)**

Chocolate amaretti creams

These sumptuous little tortes are amazingly quick and easy to make and can be prepared well in advance and left in the fridge until the evening, making them ideal for entertaining as you can spend your time with your guests.

SERVES 4

4 amaretti biscuits (cookies), crushed

250 g/9 oz plain (semi-sweet) chocolate

30 ml/2 tbsp Amaretto liqueur

30 ml/2 tbsp glycerine

300 ml/½ pt/1½ cups double (heavy) cream

TO SERVE

Single (light) cream

1 Line the bases of four ramekins (custard cups) with greaseproof (waxed) paper and divide the crushed amaretti biscuits among the dishes.

2 Gently melt the chocolate with the liqueur and glycerine in a bowl over a pan of hot water and allow to cool slightly. Whip the cream until softly peaking.

3 Stir 30 ml/2 tbsp of the cream into the chocolate mixture to soften it, then add the rest of the cream and fold in until well blended.

4 Pour into the ramekins and level the surfaces. Chill for at least 45 minutes.

5 When ready to serve, run a knife around the edge of each ramekin, cover with a plate and invert, turning the torte out on to the plate. Remove the paper and serve with a jug of single cream.

Preparation and cooking time 15 minutes plus chilling

DESSERTS

Photograph opposite:
Whisky Oranges with Honeyed Cream (see page 132)
with Lacy Caramel Webs (see page 134)

Almond pear flan

Almonds and pears are one of those classic combinations that work well in all sorts of recipes. Here they are presented in a rich, golden flan on a base of shortcrust pastry. The apricot jam gives it a lovely glazed finish.

SERVES 6

225 g/8 oz shortcrust pastry (basic pie crust)

75 g/3 oz/⅓ cup unsalted (sweet) butter

75 g/3 oz/⅓ cup caster (superfine) sugar

75 g/3 oz/¾ cup ground almonds

25 g/1 oz/¼ cup plain (all-purpose) flour

1 whole egg, beaten

1 egg yolk

2 ripe pears, peeled, cored and cut into even slices

30 ml/2 tbsp apricot jam (conserve)

TO SERVE
Single (light) cream

1 Line a greased 25 cm/10 in flan dish (pie pan) with the pastry (paste) and chill while preparing the filling.

2 Beat together the butter and sugar until light and fluffy, then mix in the ground almonds, flour, beaten egg and egg yolk. Put all of this mixture into the flan dish, level with a spatula and arrange the pear slices on top, pressing them down slightly.

3 Bake in a preheated oven at 180°C/350°F/gas 4/fan oven 160°C for 45–50 minutes until the flan is golden and firm to the touch.

4 Bring the jam to the boil with 15 ml/1 tbsp of water in a small pan, stirring with a wooden spoon. Remove from the heat and sieve (strain), then use to glaze the flan while it is still warm.

5 Serve with cream.

Preparation and cooking time About 1 hour

Hints and variations You could add a little sugar to your pastry if you like, or bind it with egg for a richer base.

Chocolate and pear pie

This pie is best made in advance, then reheated when ready to eat. The flavour is fullest when it's just warm. Chocolates and almonds make a great combination, complemented by the fresh flavour of the pears.

SERVES 8

700 g/1½ lb puff pastry (paste)

75 g/3 oz/⅓ cup unsalted (sweet) butter

75 g/3 oz/⅓ cup caster (superfine) sugar

1 egg

150 ml/¼ pt/⅔ cup soured (dairy sour) cream

100 g/4 oz/1 cup self-raising (self-rising) flour

2.5 ml/½ tsp ground ginger

15 ml/1 tbsp cocoa (unsweetened chocolate) powder

25 g/1 oz/¼ cup ground almonds

425 g/15 oz/1 large can of pear halves, drained, reserving the juice

TO GLAZE
A little milk, egg yolk and caster sugar

1 Cut the pastry in half and roll out to form rounds, one 20 cm/8 in in diameter, the other 23 cm/9 in. Place the small round on a greased baking (cookie) sheet.

2 Beat together the butter and sugar until pale and fluffy, then beat in the egg and stir in the soured cream, flour, ginger, cocoa and ground almonds.

3 Spread this mixture on to the smaller round of pastry, leaving a narrow border all around the edge. Top with the pears. Brush the edge with a little milk or cream. Place the larger pastry round on top and press the edges together to seal. Knock up with the back of a knife.

4 Decorate the top with a sharp knife, brush with milk and egg yolk and sprinkle with sugar.

5 Bake in a preheated oven at 200°C/400°F/gas 6/fan oven 180°C for 40–45 minutes.

Preparation and cooking time About 1 hour

DESSERTS

Baked apples with almond

This delicious dessert can be served either warm or cold, but whichever way you choose, don't forget that jug of cream to pour over the top. I use eating apples because they tend to keep their shape better than cooking apples.

SERVES 4

450 g/1 lb green eating (dessert) apples

75 g/3 oz/⅓ cup butter or margarine

100 g/4 oz/½ cup caster (superfine) sugar

50 g/2 oz/½ cup ground almonds

1 egg, beaten

TO DECORATE

A few flaked (slivered) almonds

TO SERVE

Single (light) cream

1 Peel, core and slice the apples and cook them in a pan or in the microwave until softened slightly. Place them in a shallow baking dish.

2 Melt the butter or margarine and add the sugar and ground almonds. Stir together to mix.

3 Add the beaten egg and mix well. Spread this mixture on top of the apples and sprinkle with the flaked almonds.

4 Bake in a preheated oven at 190°C/375°F/gas 5/fan oven 170°C for 30 minutes until the top is golden brown.

5 Serve with a jug of single cream.

Preparation and cooking time 40 minutes

Fruit sabayon

A sabayon is usually served as an accompaniment to fruit puddings, but this one is part of the dessert and finished under a hot grill like a brûlée. You can vary the fruit you use to suit what is available.

SERVES 4

3 egg yolks, beaten

50 g/2 oz/¼ cup caster (superfine) sugar, plus extra for sprinkling

Grated zest of ½ lemon

150 ml/¼ pt/⅔ cup dry white wine

60 ml/4 tbsp single (light) cream

225 g/8 oz strawberries, hulled and sliced if large

3 peaches, skinned, stoned (pitted) and sliced

1 Beat the egg yolks and sugar together in a heatproof bowl; add the lemon zest and wine. Set the bowl over a pan of simmering water and continue beating until the sauce is smooth and has thickened. Gradually stir in the cream and whisk for a minute until well combined.

2 Arrange the fruit in a shallow flameproof dish and pour the sauce over.

3 Sprinkle a little sugar on top.

4 Place under a grill (broiler), preheated to the highest setting, until golden.

5 Serve at once.

Preparation and cooking time 10–12 minutes

Meringue peaches

These peaches look very pretty and make a light and fruity end to any meal. I often serve this dish when I am using an egg yolk in a main-course recipe as I hate to waste anything.

SERVES 4

4 canned peach halves

4 amaretti biscuits (cookies)

60 ml/4 tbsp orange liqueur

1 egg white

50 g/2 oz/¼ cup caster (superfine) sugar

25 g/1 oz/¼ cup flaked (slivered) almonds

A little icing (confectioners') sugar, for dusting

1 Drain the peach halves and dry on kitchen paper (paper towels). Place, hollow sides up, on a greased baking (cookie) sheet.

2 Put an amaretti biscuit inside each one. Drizzle the liqueur over.

3 Whisk the egg white until stiff, then gradually whisk in the sugar.

4 Using a teaspoon, top the peaches with the meringue mixture, then sprinkle with the almonds.

5 Bake in a preheated oven at 200°C/400°F/gas 6/fan oven 180°C until the meringue is pale golden brown.

6 Dust lightly with icing sugar and serve at once.

Preparation and cooking time 15–20 minutes

Hints and variations Try using small squares of chocolate or ginger cake instead of the amaretti biscuits.

Coffee cream syllabub

'Syllabub' is such a wonderfully descriptive word: it really sounds like something delectable, rich and delicious – which is just what these desserts are.

SERVES 4

300 ml/½ pt/1¼ cups double (heavy) cream

1 liqueur glass of coffee liqueur

50 g/2 oz/¼ cup caster (superfine) sugar

5 ml/1 tsp instant coffee powder

TO DECORATE
Grated chocolate

1 Whip all the ingredients together until thick, then pour into wineglasses or ramekins (custard cups).

2 Chill until required. Serve with grated chocolate sprinkled on top.

Preparation time 5 minutes plus chilling

Creamy chocolate flan

This creamy white chocolate flan with its crisp, honeyed base can be made in advance and chilled until required. It makes a delicious dessert, or is great served with coffee or cups of steaming hot chocolate.

SERVES 8

275 g/10 oz/2½ cups crushed chocolate digestive biscuits (graham crackers)

100 g/4 oz/½ cup unsalted (sweet) butter, melted

15 ml/1 tbsp clear honey

600 ml/1 pt/2½ cups milk

6 egg yolks

100 g/4 oz/½ cup caster (superfine) sugar

25 g/1 oz/¼ cup cornflour (cornstarch)

225 g/8 oz/2 cups best-quality white chocolate, broken up

TO DECORATE
75 g/3 oz/¾ cup white chocolate, grated

Drinking (sweetened) chocolate powder

1 Mix together the crushed biscuits, butter and honey.

2 Press into the base and up the sides of a deep 20 cm/8 in loose-bottomed cake tin (pan).

3 Chill until set.

4 Mix a little of the milk with the egg yolks, sugar and cornflour until smooth.

5 Pour the remainder of the milk into a saucepan and bring to the boil, then pour on to the milk and egg yolk mixture and blend well. Return to the pan and stir over the heat until smooth and thick.

6 Remove from the heat and add the chocolate pieces, stirring until melted. Allow the mixture to cool slightly, then spoon into the biscuit flan case (pie shell).

7 Leave to cool completely, then transfer to a serving plate and chill. Scatter the grated chocolate over the filling, then dust lightly with the drinking chocolate powder.

Preparation and cooking time 15 minutes plus cooling and chilling

Frozen coffee crunch soufflés

These luscious individual soufflés must be made in advance to allow time for freezing, although that makes them ideal for entertaining. Transfer them to the fridge to soften slightly while you serve the main course.

SERVES 4

2 egg whites

175 g/6 oz/³⁄₄ cup caster (superfine) sugar

Boiling water

7.5 ml/1¹⁄₂ tsp instant coffee powder

15 ml/1 tbsp orange liqueur, such as Grand Marnier

375 ml/13 fl oz/1¹⁄₂ cups double (heavy) cream

12 amaretti biscuits (cookies), crushed

TO DECORATE

A little icing (confectioners') sugar

4 toasted almonds

1 Line four ramekins (custard cups) with greaseproof (waxed) paper 'collars' to stand 5 cm/2 in above the rims.

2 Whisk the egg whites until stiff in a large bowl.

3 In a small pan, dissolve the sugar in 90 ml/6 tbsp of boiling water, then boil for 3 minutes without stirring. Pour this caramel on to the egg whites in a thin stream, whisking at high speed until cool.

3 Dissolve the coffee in 7.5 ml/1¹⁄₂ tsp of boiling water, then stir in the liqueur. Whisk this mixture into the egg whites.

4 Whip the cream until softly peaking and fold into the egg white mixture. Pour into the ramekins (it should half-fill each one) and sprinkle with a thick layer of crushed amaretti biscuits. Top with the egg white mixture to 2.5 cm/1 in above the rims. Freeze for at least 2 hours, then remove the collars and coat the raised edges with the remaining crushed biscuits.

5 Dust with icing sugar and decorate each with a toasted almond before serving.

Preparation and cooking time 20 minutes plus freezing

Coffee torte with praline

I like this sort of recipe, which can be prepared in stages as and when I have the time. I usually make the praline the day before I need it – it's good to have one less job to do when putting together your dinner!

SERVES 8

175 g/6 oz/1½ cups blanched hazelnuts (filberts)

225 g/8 oz/1 cup caster (superfine) sugar

600 ml/1 pt/2½ cups double (heavy) cream

15 ml/1 tbsp instant coffee powder

30 ml/2 tbsp almond or coffee liqueur

3 packets of sponge (lady) fingers

A cup of weak black coffee

1 Toast the hazelnuts in a dry frying pan (skillet) for a few minutes, shaking the pan continuously so that the nuts become brown all over. Add 175 g/6 oz/¾ cup of the sugar, stirring all the time, until it melts into a liquid caramel. Ensure the nuts are well coated with the caramel and then pour on to a sheet of non-stick baking parchment and leave until completely cold. Break into pieces, reserve some for decoration, and grind up the rest in a food processor.

2 Whisk the double cream with the remaining sugar, the instant coffee and the chosen liqueur.

3 Dip the sponge fingers in the black coffee and use to line the base of an 18 cm/7 in loose-based square cake tin (pan). Follow with a layer of coffee cream and a sprinkling of the praline. Continue layering and finish with a thick layer of coffee cream, reserving about one-third for spreading round the sides later. Chill for at least half an hour before turning out.

4 When chilled, turn out of the tin and spread the remaining coffee cream around the sides of the cake and top with the reserved chunky pieces of praline.

Preparation time 20 minutes plus cooling and chilling

Brandy chocolate roulade

This roulade is best served chilled so allow a little time when you are planning your menu. It can be frozen for up to 3 months, then thawed at room temperature before serving – it will take about 2 hours.

SERVES 8

175 g/6 oz/1¼ cups plain (semi-sweet) chocolate, broken up

30 ml/2 tbsp hot water

175 g/6 oz/¾ cup caster (superfine) sugar, plus extra for dusting

5 eggs, separated

FOR THE FILLING

150 ml/¼ pt/⅔ cup double (heavy) cream

150 ml/¼ pt/⅔ cup soured (dairy sour) cream

30 ml/2 tbsp brandy

TO DECORATE

Chocolate curls

1 Line a 23 x 33 cm/9 x 13 in Swiss roll tin (jelly roll pan) with lightly oiled greaseproof (waxed) paper, cut large enough to extend slightly above the sides.

2 In a small pan, melt the chocolate and stir in the hot water and sugar. Whisk in the egg yolks.

3 Whisk the egg whites until stiff and fold into the chocolate mix. Pour into the prepared tin.

4 Bake in a preheated oven at 200°C/400°F/gas 6/fan oven 180°C for 15 minutes. Leave to cool in the tin for at least 2 hours.

5 Meanwhile, whip the double cream until softly peaking, then fold in the soured cream and brandy.

6 When the roulade is cold, invert it on to some greaseproof paper, dusted with caster sugar. Remove the lining paper and trim the edges. Spread the filling over, roll up and decorate with chocolate curls. Chill before serving.

Preparation and cooking time 30 minutes plus cooling and chilling

Poached pears with hot fudge sauce

I think this combination of the fruit with a lovely buttery sauce is unbeatable. Certainly, whenever I serve it to my guests, there is a lot of plate-scraping and longing looks at the sauce jug!

SERVES 6

6 firm pears, peeled and cored

600 ml/1 pt/2½ cups white wine

50 g/2 oz/¼ cup caster (superfine) sugar

15 ml/1 tbsp lemon juice

50 g/2 oz/¼ cup unsalted (sweet) butter

45 ml/3 tbsp soft brown sugar

45 ml/3 tbsp golden (light corn) syrup

30 ml/2 tbsp single (light) cream

TO DECORATE
90 ml/6 tbsp blueberries or other fruit of your choice

1 Poach the pears with the wine, caster sugar and 2 tsp/10 ml of the lemon juice for about 20–25 minutes.

2 Melt the butter, brown sugar and golden syrup together, then add the cream and the remainder of the lemon juice and heat through.

3 Pour the sauce over the pears and scatter the berries on top for added colour. Serve immediately.

Preparation and cooking time 35–40 minutes

Whisky oranges with honeyed cream

This dessert can be made a couple of days in advance so that the flavours have time to mingle with each other. The cream is from a traditional Scottish dessert recipe that usually includes oatmeal as well. See photograph opposite page 121.

SERVES 8

200 g/7 oz/scant 1 cup granulated sugar

150 ml/¼ pt/⅔ cup water

75 ml/5 tbsp Scotch whisky

8 oranges

FOR THE HONEYED CREAM
450 ml/¾ pt/2 cups double (heavy) cream

45 ml/3 tbsp clear honey

45 ml/3 tbsp Scotch whisky

TO SERVE
Lacy Caramel Webs (page 134)

1 Stir the granulated sugar and water in a small pan over a low heat until the sugar dissolves. Bring to the boil, then reduce the heat and simmer for 2 minutes. Remove from the heat, add the whisky and leave to cool.

2 Remove all the rind and pith from the oranges and cut into segments, cutting between the membranes. Put the segments into a bowl and pour the syrup over.

3 Whip the double cream until it is softly peaking. Put the honey and whisky into a bowl and stir until well blended. Gradually whisk into the cream until thick. Chill until ready to serve.

4 Spoon the oranges and syrup into eight small glass bowls and top with the honeyed cream. Serve with Lacy Caramel Webs.

Preparation time 25 minutes plus chilling

Chocolate and ginger trifle

This luscious dessert is perfect after a light meal. The flavours need to have time to develop, so you should prepare it in advance and leave in the fridge for 3–4 hours before needed. Use the ginger syrup from the jar of stem ginger.

SERVES 4

225 g/8 oz/1 cup Mascarpone cheese

250 ml/8 fl oz/1 cup crème fraîche

75 g/3 oz/¹⁄₃ cup granulated sugar

175 g/6 oz chocolate brownies, sliced

50 ml/2 fl oz/¹⁄₄ cup ginger syrup

A little ginger wine or brandy (optional)

15 g/¹⁄₂ oz/1 tbsp finely chopped stem ginger

150 g/5 oz/1¹⁄₄ cups plain (semi-sweet) chocolate, chopped

15 g/¹⁄₂ oz/2 tbsp drinking (sweetened) chocolate powder

1 Stir the Mascarpone to soften it, then add the crème fraîche and sugar. Beat the mixture well until it is smooth.

2 Press half the brownie slices into the bottom of a glass trifle bowl, then drizzle half the ginger syrup and alcohol, if liked, over the slices. Top with half the Mascarpone mixture. Sprinkle on half the stem ginger and half of the chopped chocolate and cover with all of the drinking chocolate powder.

3 Repeat the process, ending with the second half of the chopped chocolate.

4 Chill for 3–4 hours before serving.

Preparation time 5 minutes plus chilling

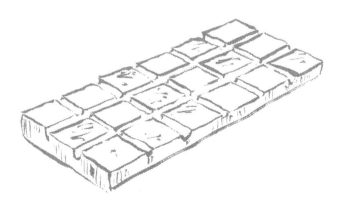

Champagne chocolate flutes with lacy caramel webs

These are absolutely divine. Do remember to plan ahead with regard to space in the fridge for the flutes, as the mixture takes time to set. It's well worth the extra time. You can use the lacy caramel webs on other desserts too (see photograph opposite page 121).

SERVES 4

100 g/4 oz/1 cup plain (semi-sweet) chocolate, broken up

100 g/4 oz/1 cup white chocolate, broken up

2 small crunchy biscuits (cookies)

50 g/2 oz seedless green grapes, peeled

120 ml/4 fl oz/½ cup champagne or sparkling white wine

3 eggs, separated

60 ml/4 tbsp Mascarpone cheese

FOR THE LACY CARAMEL WEBS
100 g/4 oz/½ cup caster (superfine) sugar

75 ml/5 tbsp water

1 Melt the plain and white chocolates in separate bowls set over pans of simmering water.

2 Crumble the biscuits and sprinkle into four champagne flutes. Add the peeled grapes, then pour 15 ml/1 tbsp of champagne into each glass.

3 When the bowls of chocolate have melted, let them cool for 5 minutes before tipping half of the egg yolks into each and stirring until glossy. Sometimes the mixture can go a bit stiff at this stage but do not worry – it will soften again once you add the cream.

4 Whisk the egg whites until softly peaking. Stir the Mascarpone to soften it and then add the egg whites and the remaining champagne, mixing well. Divide this mixture between the bowls of chocolate and stir each until smooth. Chill for 10 minutes.

5 Spoon the chocolate mixtures alternately into the champagne flutes, to give contrasting layers. Chill for 3 hours.

6 In a small pan, heat the sugar with the water until dissolved, bring to the boil, then reduce the heat and simmer until it turns a dark gold. Remove from the heat immediately – do not allow it to go brown. Cool for a minute, then drizzle lines of the mixture on to baking parchment to make four 'webs' like spun gold.

7 Serve the chocolate desserts with the webs on top.

Preparation time 20 minutes plus chilling

Apple and orange brûlée

Fruit brûlées are always a popular way to end a meal – my guests seem to love the contrast of the sharp fresh fruit and the rich sweet topping. I like them because they are very easy to prepare!

Serves 4

175 ml/6 fl oz/³/₄ cup crème fraîche

2 small eating (dessert) apples, cored and diced

2 small oranges, peeled and chopped

100 g/4 oz/¹/₂ cup soft brown or granulated sugar

1 Mix all the ingredients except the sugar well together and place in a shallow flameproof dish. Chill well.

2 Spread the sugar on top of the fruit mixture and put under a hot grill (broiler) for about 2 minutes until the sugar caramelises. Chill until needed. Alternatively, add a drop of water to the granulated sugar and put in the microwave in a heatproof dish and cook on High until it forms a light yellow toffee. Pour over the fruit mixture and chill until required.

3 To serve, bring to the table straight from the fridge and tap the toffee with a metal spoon. This cracks the top and makes it easy to serve.

Preparation and cooking time 5 minutes plus chilling

Hints and variations You can use a mixture of double (heavy) cream and thick plain yoghurt instead of the crème fraîche if you prefer.

Fresh peppered oranges with yoghurt sauce

This unusual summery pudding is very light, making it ideal after a rich main course. It sounds slightly unusual – with its hot seasoning and spices – but they complement the oranges really well.

SERVES 4

4 oranges, peeled

Salt and freshly ground black or white pepper

A few roasted cumin seeds, ground

A little cayenne

250 ml/8 fl oz/1 cup plain yoghurt

5 ml/1 tsp finely grated fresh root ginger

20 ml/4 tsp caster (superfine) sugar

1 Cut the oranges into 5–6 slices and then cut each slice in half.

2 Sprinkle one side very lightly with salt, pepper, cumin and cayenne. Arrange the slices in a slightly overlapping circle on each of four plates, leaving a gap in the middle. Cover with clingfilm (plastic wrap) and chill.

3 Blend the yoghurt with the ginger, sugar and a pinch each of salt, pepper, cumin and cayenne until smooth and creamy.

4 When ready to serve, place a spoonful of this mixture in the centre of each circle of orange slices.

Preparation time 10 minutes plus chilling

Lemon curd mousse

This light, fluffy mousse provides a perfect finish to a meal. It is particularly refreshing after a rich main course, with the sharpness of the lemons to cut through any richness in the previous dishes.

SERVES 6

7.5 ml/1½ tsp gelatine

100 g/4 oz/½ cup caster (superfine) sugar

3 eggs, separated

Grated zest and juice of 2 small lemons

65 g/2½ oz/scant ⅓ cup butter

1 Sprinkle the gelatine on to 30 ml/2 tbsp of water and leave to soften.

2 Reserve 25 g/1 oz/2 tbsp of the sugar and whisk the remainder with the egg yolks until thick and pale.

3 Put the lemon zest, lemon juice and butter in a saucepan and bring to the boil. Add the soaked gelatine, then put into a food processor or blender with the yolk mixture and run the machine for 1½–2 minutes.

4 In a large bowl, whisk the egg whites until just peaking. Whisk in the remaining sugar and then fold in the hot lemon mixture.

5 Turn into individual glass dishes and chill for 4–6 hours before serving.

Preparation time 10 minutes plus chilling

Hints and variations This is even better if you serve it sprinkled with grated plain (semi-sweet) chocolate.

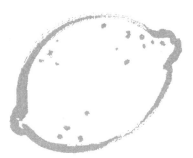

Iced fruit parfait

The flavour and colour of the parfait is enhanced by making the coulis with bilberries, but raspberries will do just as well if you can't get hold of them in your local greengrocer or supermarket.

SERVES 8

200 g/7 oz bilberries

25 g/1 oz/2 tbsp caster (superfine) sugar

150 ml/¹/₄ pt/²/₃ cup double (heavy) cream

4 egg whites

100 g/4 oz/²/₃ cup icing (confectioners') sugar

450 g/1 lb strawberries, crushed

TO DECORATE
Fresh fruit

1 First make your coulis: put the bilberries into a saucepan with the caster sugar and cook over a high heat until the sugar dissolves. Bring to the boil, then reduce the heat and simmer for 2 minutes. Use a wooden spoon to press the fruit through a fine nylon sieve (strainer) into a bowl and leave to cool.

2 Line a 20 cm/8 in springform cake tin (pan) with baking parchment.

3 Whip the cream until firm.

4 Whisk the egg whites until stiff, then gradually whisk in the icing sugar.

5 Fold together the whisked egg whites, strawberries and cream until well combined, then stir 45 ml/3 tbsp of the coulis gently through the mixture to give a marbled appearance – do not mix completely.

6 Spoon into the prepared cake tin and freeze for at least 4 hours.

7 When ready to serve, peel off the baking parchment, cut the parfait into wedges and decorate with fresh fruit and the remaining coulis.

Preparation time 10 minutes plus cooling and freezing

Hints and variations You may be able to buy jars of fruit coulis from the supermarket – it is also sold in frozen sachets. If you prefer individual parfaits, freeze the mixture in ramekins (custard cups).

Raspberry pavlova

*The contrast between the lovely fresh raspberries and the sweet meringue and
whipped cream is perfection itself. This is a dessert to make when you have used
egg yolks in another recipe so nothing is wasted.*

SERVES 8

4 egg whites

**225 g/8 oz/1 cup caster
(superfine) sugar**

15 ml/1 tbsp cornflour (cornstarch)

1.5 ml/¼ tsp vanilla essence (extract)

10 ml/2 tsp vinegar

FOR THE FILLING
**450 ml/¾ pt/2 cups double (heavy)
cream, whipped**

350 g/12 oz fresh raspberries

1 Whisk the egg whites until stiff, then gradually add the sugar, still
whisking all the time.

2 Stir in the remaining ingredients.

3 Spoon the mixture on to a greased baking (cookie) sheet, preferably
lined with non-stick baking parchment. Bake in a preheated oven at
150°C/300°F/gas 2/fan oven 135°C for 1½ hours.

4 When cool, fill the centre with the whipped cream and raspberries.

Preparation and cooking time About 1¾ hours

Hints and variations You can prepare the meringue in advance,
whenever you have the time to spare, and then keep it covered in
foil or in an airtight container until required. The dessert can then be
assembled in minutes.

139

Tom's chocolate gateau

This is a really moist mix, so take care when slicing it in two before filling as it tends to crumble easily. The black cherry jam makes the flavour highly reminiscent of Black Forest gâteau.

SERVES 6

175 g/6 oz/1½ cups plain (all-purpose) flour

175 g/6 oz/¾ cup granulated sugar

50 g/2 oz/½ cup cocoa (unsweetened chocolate) powder

2.5 ml/½ tsp salt

5 ml/1 tsp bicarbonate of soda (baking soda)

5 ml/1 tsp vanilla essence (extract)

15 ml/1 tbsp cider vinegar

120 ml/4 fl oz/½ cup sunflower oil

250 ml/8 fl oz/1 cup water

FOR THE FILLING AND TOPPING

30–45 ml/2–3 tbsp black cherry jam (conserve)

150 ml/¼ pt/⅔ cup double (heavy) cream, whipped

A little grated plain (semi-sweet) chocolate

1 Grease and line a 20 cm/8 in deep cake tin (pan).

2 Combine the flour, sugar, cocoa, salt and bicarbonate of soda. Make a well in the centre and add the vanilla, vinegar, oil and water. Mix until just blended.

3 Turn into the prepared tin. Bake in a preheated oven at 190°C/375°F/ gas 5/fan oven 170°C for 40 minutes. Leave to cool in the tin on a wire rack for 10 minutes, then turn out and leave to cool completely.

4 When cold, split carefully in two horizontally, then fill with jam and half the whipped cream. Spread the remaining cream on top and sprinkle with grated chocolate.

Preparation and cooking time 50 minutes plus cooling

Bananas with brandy caramel sauce

This is a delicious, rich dessert that can be prepared in minutes. Served in an attractive sundae glass and sprinkled with grated chocolate or nuts, it makes a really easy but impressive end to a meal.

SERVES 6

5 cm/2 in piece of cinnamon stick

Juice of 1 orange

15 ml/1 tbsp soft brown sugar

6 bananas

30 ml/2 tbsp Cointreau

FOR THE SAUCE

4 Mars bars

About 30 ml/2 tbsp water

30 ml/2 tbsp brandy

1 Put the cinnamon, orange juice and sugar in a pan over a low heat so the sugar dissolves.

2 Thickly slice the bananas diagonally and add to the pan. Cook for 2 minutes, then add the Cointreau and cook for a further 3 minutes. Put into individual glass dishes.

3 Chop the Mars bars finely, put into another pan and melt over a very low heat, adding enough water to keep the mixture runny. Add the brandy, stir until blended and pour over the bananas.

4 Serve immediately.

Preparation and cooking time 10 minutes

Hints and variations: Try the sauce poured over ice cream – it's fabulous!

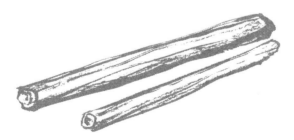

index

anchovies
anchovy cream 115
anchovy vinaigrette 115
apples
  apple and orange brûlée 135
  baked apples with almond 124
asparagus and salmon risotto 21
aubergines
aubergine rolls with basil and
  Mozzarella 79
aubergine stacks with ratatouille 84
avocados
  grilled avocados with bacon 20

bacon
  bacon-wrapped cod fillets with
    tarragon cream sauce 74
  French beans with bacon and
    spring onions 95
  grilled avocados with bacon 20
bananas with brandy caramel
  sauce 141
beans, green
  French beans with bacon and
    spring onions 95
  French beans with feta and
    sun-dried tomatoes 96
  French beans with onions and
    garlic 95
  soy garlic beans 96
  warm bean salad 94
beans, haricot
  refried beans 94
beef
  beef carpaccio with salsa
    verde 48
  braised beef fillet with pink
    peppercorns and redcurrant
    jelly 49
  fillet steaks with creamy
    mushrooms and tarragon 50

Flemish beef carbonnade with a
  garlic crust 52
Greek-style beef with feta 54
old-fashioned beef casserole
  with mustard 51
spiced beef casserole with
  orange and rum 53
broccoli
  steamed broccoli with garlic and
    mustard seeds 97
brûlées
  apple and orange brûlée 135
  hot raspberry brûlée 120

cabbage with nutmeg 97
carrots
  baby carrots with orange and
    cardamom 98
  garlic carrots and courgettes
    with lime 99
  orange and carrot soup with
    cinnamon 15
  Turkish fried carrots 98
cauliflower
  feta cauliflower with tomato
    sauce 81
  steamed cauliflower with
    almonds 99
chick peas
  spicy chick peas with spinach
    and mushrooms 80
chicken
  chicken breasts and ham with
    melted cheese 34
  chicken breasts with port and
    basil 35
  flambéed brandy chicken in a
    creamy mustard sauce 36
  golden chicken with piquant
    caper relish 29

Italian-style chicken with
  rosemary and garlic 37
lemon chicken with rosemary
  and chilli 30
mustard chicken with tarragon
  cream 31
Oriental marinated chicken with
  cumin and ginger 33
Chicken and chorizo sauté 32
chocolate
  brandy chocolate roulade 130
  champagne chocolate flutes with
    lacy caramel webs 134
  chocolate amaretti creams 121
  chocolate and ginger trifle 133
  chocolate and pear pie 123
  chocolate tart with rum 119
  creamy chocolate flan 127
  Tom's chocolate gateau 140
chorizo sausage
  chicken and chorizo
    sauté 32
  Spanish chorizo salad 25
cod
  bacon-wrapped cod fillets with
    tarragon cream sauce 74
  fruits de mer en papillote 72
  heavenly fish bake with golden
    potato topping 71
  pescada a la marina 64
coffee
  coffee cream syllabub 126
  coffee torte with praline 129
  frozen coffee crunch
    soufflés 128
courgettes
  baked courgettes with cheese
    and sweetcorn 88
  courgette patties 101
  creamed courgette soup with
    tomato and basil 18

creamy courgette bake 100
garlic carrots and courgettes
   with lime 99

diet, healthy 9
dressings and relishes 115–116
drinks, serving 10
duck
   grilled duck breasts with
     caramelised onions 40
   peppered duck breasts with
     cognac 39
   sautéed duck breasts with port
     and redcurrant 41

fennel
   baked fennel with fresh
     tomatoes 103
   braised fennel with garlic and
     cream 102
feta cheese
   feta cauliflower with tomato
     sauce 81
French beans with feta and sun-
   dried tomatoes 96
feuilletés de St Jacques 70
flans (savoury)
   sensational onion flan 76
flans (sweet)
   almond pear flan 122
   chocolate and pear pie 123
   chocolate tart with rum 119
   coffee torte with praline 129
   creamy chocolate flan 127
fruit
   fruit sabayon 125
   iced fruit parfait 138

gateau, Tom's chocolate 140
goats' cheese
   fried goats' cheese with
     walnuts 27
   leek and goats' cheese pie with
     tomato sauce 85
goulash, vegetarian 91

haddock
   pescada à la marina 64

haricot beans
   refried beans 94

kumquat and red onion
   marmalade 112

lamb
   Italian lamb with Parma ham and
     pesto 55
   marinated roast lamb with lemon
     and herbs 57
   roast leg of lamb with red wine
     and ginger 61
   roast rack of lamb with orange
     and port sauce 56
   roasted soy lamb fillets in a lime
     and garlic marinade 58
   shortcut Shrewsbury lamb 59
   tagine barrogog bis basela 60
leeks
   braised leeks in vermouth 104
   honeyed leek sauce 116
   leek and goats' cheese pie with
     tomato sauce 85
   piquant leeks with orange 104
   risotto bake with leeks and fresh
     herbs 83
lemon curd mousse 137

mackerel
   smoked mackerel salad with
     orange and dill 26
menus 8, 9, 11
meringues
   meringue peaches 126
   raspberry Pavlova 139
mousse, lemon curd 137
mushrooms
   creamy mushroom risotto with
     thyme and lemon 78
   fried mushrooms with port and
     walnuts 23
   mushroom pilaff with cashew
     nuts 92
   piquant mushrooms on garlic
     toasts 24
onions
   festive sweet and sour onions
     with passata 110

kumquat and red onion
   marmalade 112
   sensational onion flan 76
oranges
   apple and orange brûlée 135
   fresh peppered oranges with
     yoghurt sauce 136
   orange and carrot soup with
     cinnamon 15
   whisky oranges with honeyed
     cream 132

peaches, meringue 126
pears
   almond pear flan 122
   chocolate and pear pie 123
   poached pears with hot fudge
     sauce 131
peas
   fried peas with garlic 101
pies see flans
pilaff
   mushroom pilaff with cashew
     nuts 92
plaice
   Thai grilled fish with lime 73
pork
   baked pork steaks with a crisp
     nut and mustard topping 47
   Italian-style pork chops with
     Mozzarella 44
   lemon pork tenderloin with
     sherried mushrooms 46
   rolled pork tenderloin with pine
     nut stuffing 45
potatoes
   Antibes potatoes 108
   classic potatoes with cream 106
   garlic rosti 109
   gâteau de pommes de terre 82
   lemon potatoes 105
   potato and tomato gratin with
     pesto and crème fraîche 88
   potato gratin with chilli 77
   potato patties 108
   potato stacks 109
   sugar-browned potatoes 105
   Swedish potatoes 107

poultry *see* individual types
prawns
    fruits de mer en papillote 72
    ginger dip prawns 19
    gingered prawns with stir-fried
       broccoli 63
    piri piri prawns 22
    Spanish prawns with chilli and
       almonds 22
presentation 10

quail
    Moroccan-style quail with saffron
       and sultana sauce 42

raspberries
    hot raspberry brûlée 120
    raspberry Pavlova 139
ratatouille
    aubergine stacks with
       ratatouille 84
rice *see* risottos
ricotta cheese
    spinach and ricotta parcels 90
risottos
    asparagus and salmon risotto 21
    creamy mushroom risotto with
       thyme and lemon 78
    risotto bake with leeks and fresh
       herbs 83
roulade, brandy chocolate 130

sabayon, fruit 125
salads
    smoked mackerel salad with
       orange and dill 26
    Spanish chorizo salad with
       tomatoes and spring onions 25
    tabbouleh salad 86

warm bean salad 94
    warm spinach salad 111
salmon
    asparagus and salmon risotto 21
    glazed salmon with hoisin and
       ginger 65
    herb-crusted salmon with rich
       tomato sauce 66
    marinated salmon steaks with
       orange and honey 73
scallops
    feuilletés de St Jacques 70
seafood soup with fennel and
    leek 17
shallots, glazed 110
soufflés
    frozen coffee crunch soufflés 128
soup
    creamed courgette soup with
       tomato and basil 18
    fresh tomato soup with
       Mediterranean herbs 16
    orange and carrot soup with
       cinnamon 15
    seafood soup with fennel and
       leek 17
    spinach and mascarpone soup
       with croûtons 14
spinach
    creamed spinach 111
    fresh tagliatelle with a spinach
       and mushroom sauce 87
    spicy chick peas with spinach
       and mushrooms 80
    spinach and mascarpone soup
       with croutons 14
    spinach and ricotta parcels 90
    warm spinach salad 111

steak
    fillet steaks with creamy
       mushrooms and tarragon 50
storecupboard 8–9
syllabub, coffee cream 126

tabbouleh salad 86
tagine barrogog bis basela 60
tagliatelle
    fresh tagliatelle with a spinach
       and mushroom sauce 87
tarts *see* flans
tomatoes
    fresh tomato soup with
       Mediterranean herbs 16
    potato and tomato gratin with
       pesto and crème fraîche 88
    tomato salsa 116
trifle, chocolate and ginger 133
trout
    fillets of trout in Pernod sauce 68
    Sautéed trout fillets with lemon
       butter sauce 67
turkey escalopes in ginger wine
    and lemon 36
turnips
    glazed turnips with mustard 113
    orange-glazed turnips 112

vegetables
    dressing up 117
    garlic-roast vegetables with
       rosemary 89
    Italian vegetable bake 114
vegetarian goulash 91

whiting
    crisp whiting fillets with orange
       and parsley butter 69